Jesus prayed for Strength in the Garden of Gethsemane before His 6 Trials

For Youth Groups, Jesus Lovers, Church Leaders, Bible Study Groups, and Families eager for a deeper understanding of our Lord Jesus Christ
(Study Guide Included)

Debbie Dunn

FYI - Unless otherwise noted, most Biblical quotes come from either the King James Version (KJV) or the New International Version (NIV) of the Bible APP.

<u>Permissions</u>: This book or any portion thereof may not be reproduced or used in any manner without the publisher's express written permission except for using brief quotations in a book review. For copy permission, please email the author, Debbie Dunn, at moredunntales@yahoo.com. Place, in the subject line: **Jesus prayed for Strength in the Garden of Gethsemane before His 6 Trials**

<u>Disclaimer</u>: The content used in this book is intended for educational and informational purposes only.

ISBN: 9798227329714
Imprint: Independently published. Distributed by Draft 2 Digital

T.R.E.A.T. Tales Presents

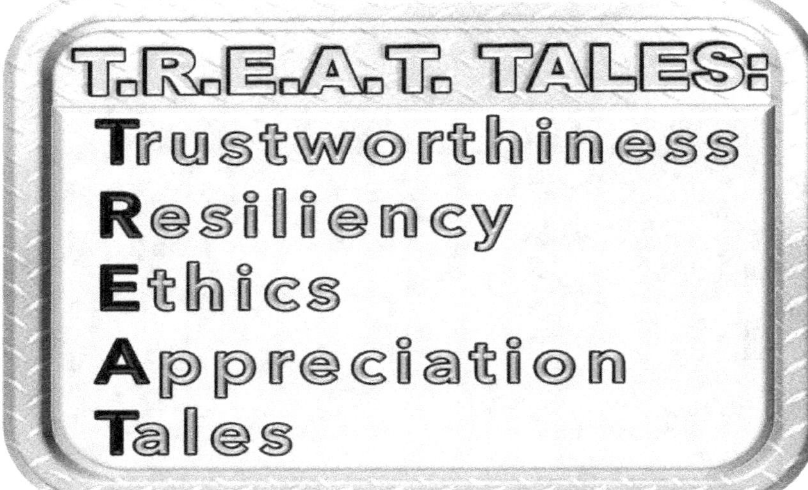

Website: https://bible-books-for-his-glory.com/index.html
Email: moredunntales@yahoo.com

About the Author: Debbie Dunn

Debbie Dunn has been a professional storyteller since 1989. She has also taught at-risk teens, served as an anti-bullying specialist, and taught elementary and middle school. In her retirement years, she indulges her love of our Lord Jesus Christ, nature, traveling, and writing as she pursues learning and exploring more about the Holy Bible.

Jesus prayed for Strength in the Garden of Gethsemane before His 6 Trials is a book crafted explicitly for youth groups, Jesus lovers, church leaders, Bible study groups, and families eager for a deeper understanding of our Lord Jesus Christ. The author, understanding the unique needs of these groups, has filled this book with conceptual color illustrations that will resonate with them and has included a study guide for their convenience.

This book describes the following points:

- After the Last Supper, on Passover Seder, Jesus took His Disciples to the Garden of Gethsemane to pray.
- Jesus prayed 3 times, "***Father, if you are willing, take this cup from me; yet not my will, but yours be done.***"
- Jesus requested Peter, John, and James to watch and pray. Three times, he found them sleeping instead.
- Jesus was so dreading the upcoming torture that He sweated blood.
- Jesus' love for all humankind (past, present, and future) exceeded His fear. He agreed to suffer unspeakable torture and pain, make atonement for all people's sins, and allow the Roman soldiers to crucify Him.
- Judas Iscariot came with armed soldiers to capture Jesus. He singled Him out by giving Jesus a kiss of betrayal.
- After Jesus' midnight arrest, He endured six trials early Friday of 30 AD:
- **1 AM**: Trial 1 of 6 at the residence of the former High Priest, Annas
- **2 AM**: Trial 2 of 6 at the residence of High Priest Caiaphas,
- As predicted, Peter denied Christ 3 times before the cock crowed.
- **3-4 AM**: Trial 3 of 6 at Sanhedrin Hall. The Jewish elders declared Jesus was guilty and deserving of death.
- Out of guilt, before hanging himself, Judas tried to return the 30 pieces of silver the Sanhedrin paid him.
- **6 AM**: Pontius Pilate presided over trial 4 of 6
- **7 AM**: King Herod presided over trial 5 of 6.
- **8 AM**: Pontius Pilate presided over trial 6 of 6.
- Pilate ordered his Roman soldiers to scourge Jesus. He allowed them to torture Jesus brutally and shove a Crown of Thorns into His skull. As a Passover tradition, the people demanded Pilate release the murderer, Barabbas, and crucify the guiltless Jesus. Pilate washed His hands of this innocent man's blood.

Fifty percent (50%) of all book sales will be donated to **Covenant House** to "***join the fight to end youth homelessness***."

FYI – This is a stand-alone book pulled from 24 sections of my 75-chapter book titled, "Jesus' Crucifixion and Resurrection foretold by 12 Biblical Prophets & Kings." Those 24 sections include:

Gethsemane Prayers & 6 Trials Book	Jesus' Crucifixion and Resurrection ... Book
Chapter 1 of this book is the same as	*Chapter 6 of my other book.*
Study Guide for Chap. 1 is the same as	*Study Guide for Chap. 6 of my other book.*
Chapter 2 of this book is the same as	*Chapter 3 of my other book*
Study Guide for Chap. 2 is the same as	*Study Guide for Chap. 3 of my other book.*
Chapter 3 of this book is the same as	*Chapter 7 of my other book.*
Chapter 4 of this book is the same as	*Chapter 8 of my other book.*
Chapter 5 of this book is the same as	*Chapter 9 of my other book.*
Chapter 6 of this book is the same as	*Chapter 10 of my other book.*
Chapter 7 of this book is the same as	*Chapter 11 of my other book*
Chapter 8 of this book is the same as	*Chapter 12 of my other book.*
Study Guide for Ch. 3-8 is the same as	*Study Guide for Ch. 7-12 of my other book.*
Chapter 9 of this book is the same as	*Chapter 13 of my other book.*
Chapter 10 of this book is the same as	*Chapter 14 of my other book.*
Chapter 11 of this book is the same as	*Chapter 15 of my other book.*
Study Guide for Ch. 9-11 is the same as	*Study Guide for Ch. 12-15 of my other book.*
Chapter 12 of this book is the same as	*Chapter 16 of my other book*
Study Guide for Ch. 12 is the same as	*Study Guide for Ch. 16 of my other book.*
Chapter 13 of this book is the same as	*Chapter 17 of my other book*
Chapter 14 of this book is the same as	*Chapter 18 of my other book*
Chapter 15 of this book is the same as	*Chapter 19 of my other book*
Chapter 16 of this book is the same as	*Chapter 20 of my other book*
Study Guide for Ch. 13-16 is same as	*Study Guide for Ch. 17-20 of my other book.*
Chapter 17 is the same as	*Chapter 74 of my other book.*
Chapter 18 is a shortened Bibliography	*found in Chapter 75 of my other book.*

PRAYING FOR STRENGTH IN THE GARDEN OF GETHSEMANE

Jesus told Disciples to wait while He prayed.

Examine 4 Gospels for Clues (KJV)

Matthew 26:36	Mark 14:32	Luke 22:39-40	John 18:1
36 Then cometh Jesus with them unto a place called Gethsemane, and saith unto the disciples, Sit ye here, while I go and pray yonder.	**32** And they came to a place which was named Gethsemane: and he saith to his disciples, Sit ye here, while I shall pray.	**39** And he came out, and went, as he was wont, to the mount of Olives; and his disciples also followed him. **40** And when he was at the place, he said unto them, Pray that ye enter not into temptation	**1** When Jesus had spoken these words, he went forth with his disciples over the brook Cedron, where was a garden, into the which he entered, and his disciples.

Is the Mount of Olives, as referenced in Luke 22:39 near the Garden of Gethsemane, as referenced in both Matthew 26:36 and Mark 14:32?

  **Examine 4 Gospels for Clues (KJV)** 

Matthew 26:37-38	Mark 14:33-34	Luke 22:41	John
37 And he took with him Peter and the two sons of Zebedee, and began to be sorrowful and very heavy. **38** "My soul is exceeding sorrowful, even unto death: tarry ye here, and watch with me."	**33** And he taketh with him Peter and James and John, and began to be sore amazed, and to be very heavy; **34** And saith unto them, My soul is exceeding sorrowful unto death: tarry ye here, and watch.	**41** And he was withdrawn from them about a stone's cast, and kneeled down, and prayed.	No Reference to this Topic.  PRAYER

What was going through the minds of Peter, John, and James as they saw Jesus practically stagger away from them? The whole evening made them feel more emotions than they were equipped to handle. They probably looked at each other like, "Uh, ..., what should we do now?"

John probably reminded them that Jesus asked them to pray. They each found a tree, dropped to their knees, and prayed. They might have felt uncertain about how to compose or direct their prayers as Jesus had said so many unsettling things.

In **Mark 14:40** and **Matthew 26:43**, we learned that "*their eyes were heavy.*" In **Luke 22:45**, he stated that Jesus "*found them sleeping for sorrow.*"

After praying, they settled comfortably, leaning against their respective trees. We get another clue from **Luke 22:41**, which stated that Jesus "*was withdrawn from them about a stone's throw.*" That meant they could hear Jesus crying and wailing. Peter, John, and James probably found themselves crying from sympathy, love, confusion, depression, and feelings of abandonment. Despite themselves, their eyelids grew so heavy that, try as they might, they could not manage to remain awake.

Jesus' 1st of 3 Prayers for Strength

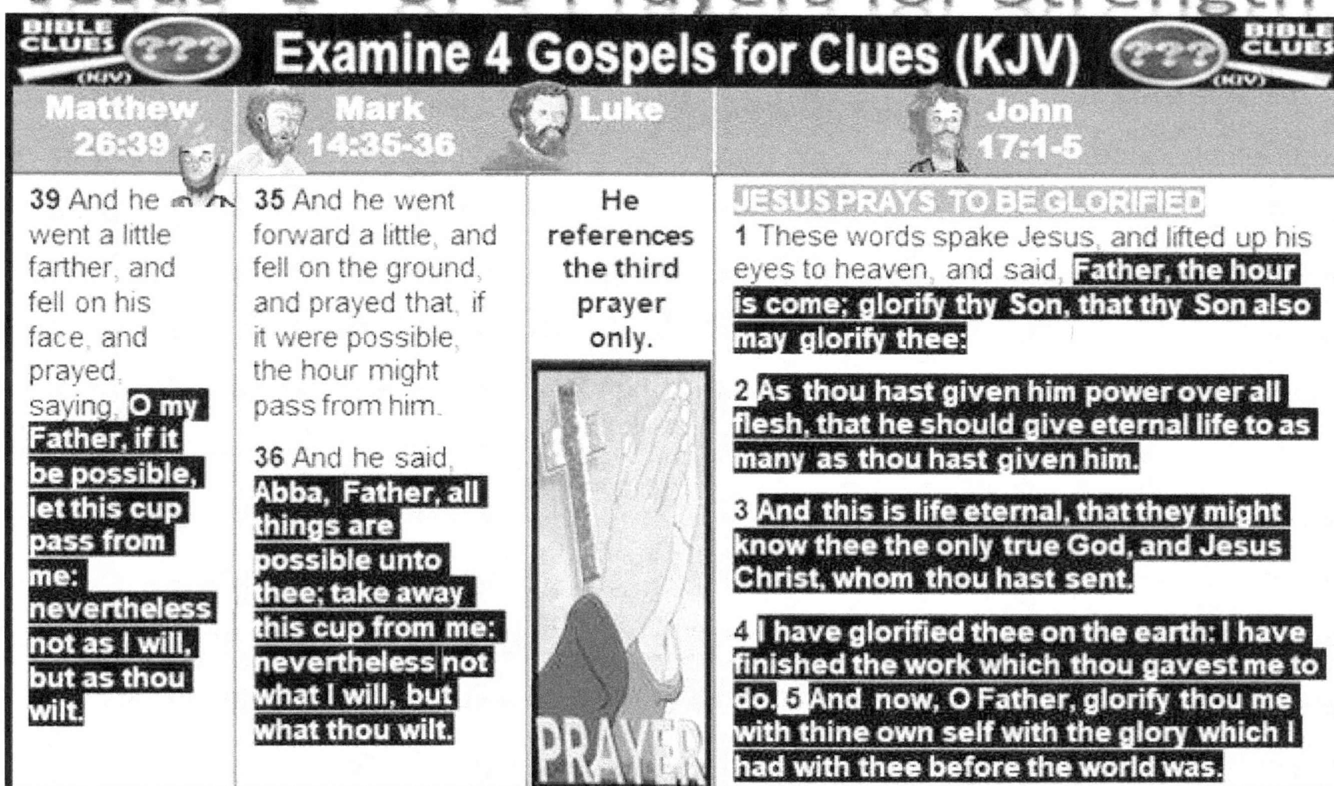

Mark 14:35 And he went forward a little, and fell on the ground, and prayed that, if it were possible, the hour might pass from him. 36 And he said, "Abba, Father, all things are possible unto thee; take away this cup from me: nevertheless not what I will, but what thou wilt."

"

Beyond the Bible verses describing what happened in the Garden of Gethsemane, what was Jesus feeling that night? Books written, movies made, and sermons preached about the life of Jesus provide us with several clues.

The men and women who probably come closest to Jesus' mindset are Veterans who went through active duty in war-torn areas. They were all too aware that each day lived might be their last or that they might come home with severe wounds or lost limbs. With those words, I thank each Veteran for their great sacrifice to serve our country or your country of origin. Where it differs is that each Veteran had a chance to remain alive and unhurt, at least physically. As for Jesus, He was born to be a slaughtered, sacrificial Lamb.

Here is my best guess of what was happening behind the scenes.

Yes, Jesus was entirely God, but He also was fully man. During that lifetime, He had the same five physical senses that all humankind possess. The Son of God could feel hunger, thirst, and pain. As God, He already mentally witnessed every moment of the excruciating torture, humiliation, and death that would happen. As a man, he would not be shielded or numbed from even one moment of agonizing pain. To save all of humankind, He would have to experience being pushed around, slapped, punched, having much of his beard yanked out, and feel the bite of the thorns pressing into his scalp as they beat His head, pressing in those spikes even more deeply. He would have to endure being scourged 39 to 40 times with that whip, called a flagellum, that contained bits of bone, glass, and metal that would not only score His back but extract large sections of skin and upper and possibly lower dermis. He would have to drag the instrument of His death, the cross, which could have weighed about 165 pounds. He would have to feel the nails pounded into His wrists and ankles. The only physical pain He would not have to experience was the spear stabbing His side since He would already be dead. The list goes on. But we all get the general idea.

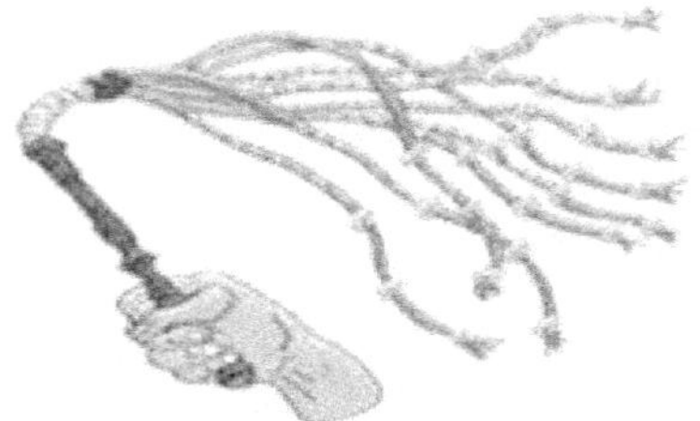
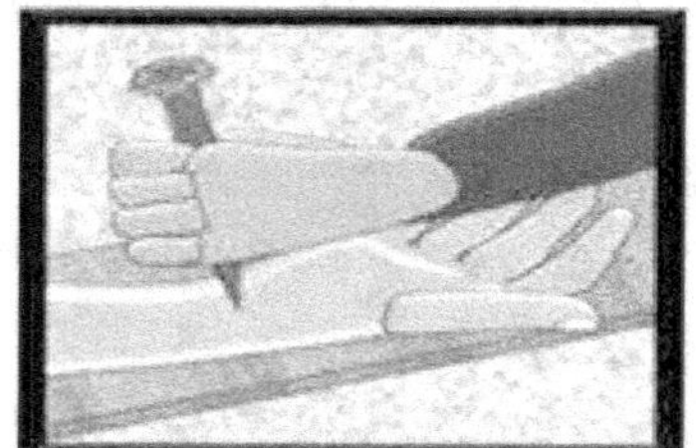
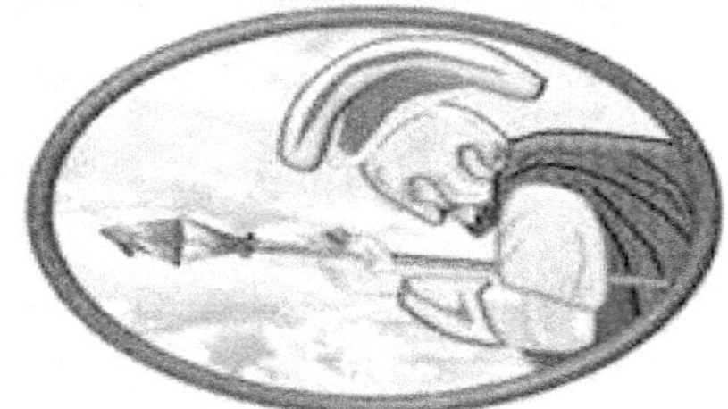

Yes, Jesus was born knowing He would have to be the sinless sacrificial Lamb to save all humans. It is one thing to know something with your head and another thing to face it in reality.

Given all that, it is no wonder that He cried out to God with the request to find another way for humankind to be Saved without all the excruciating torture.

Got Questions.org stated, **"Conservatively, Jesus fulfilled at least 300 prophecies in His earthly ministry."** See the Bibliography or Google the title, *'How many prophecies did Jesus fulfill?'* should you wish to read the Biblical verses pointing to the life of Jesus.

I'm sure Father God, the God of meticulous details, reminded Jesus of how carefully they planned out His earthly campaign. I also believe Jesus had every intention of going through with their plans. It was only human to at least ask the question in case a different answer could suddenly present itself. After all, the human side of Him was experiencing great fear, dread, and terror of what was soon to take place.

Jesus found trio sleeping instead of praying.

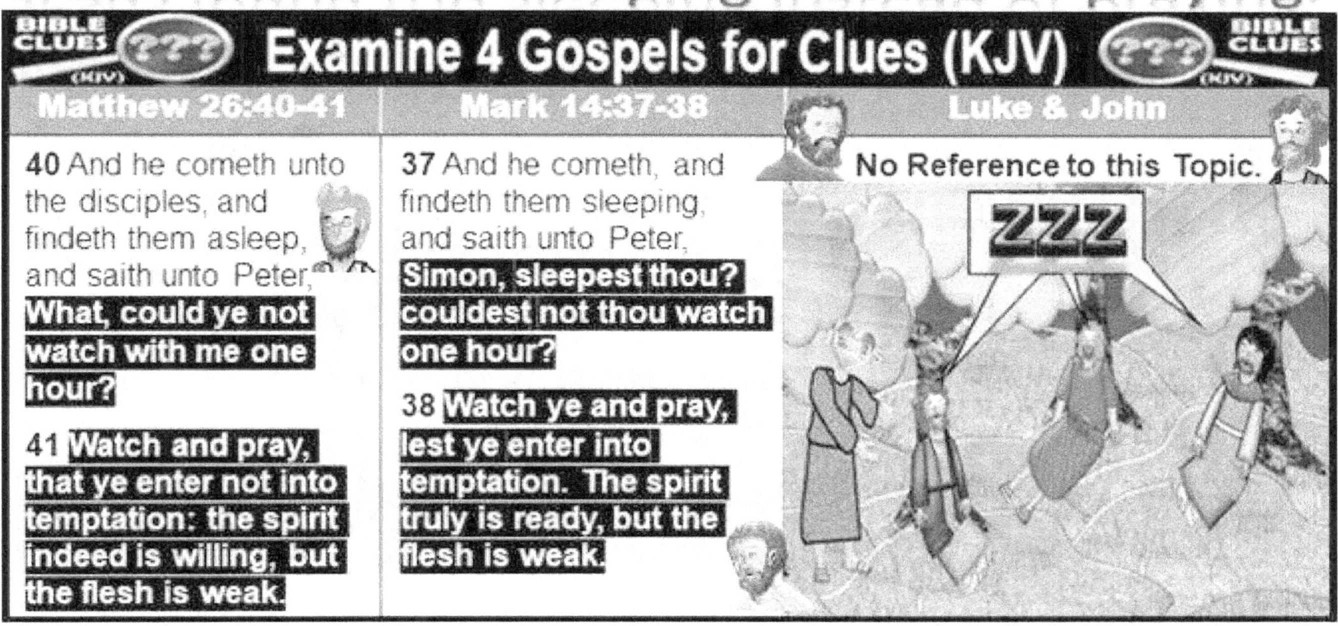

Matthew 26:40 And he cometh unto the disciples, and findeth them asleep.

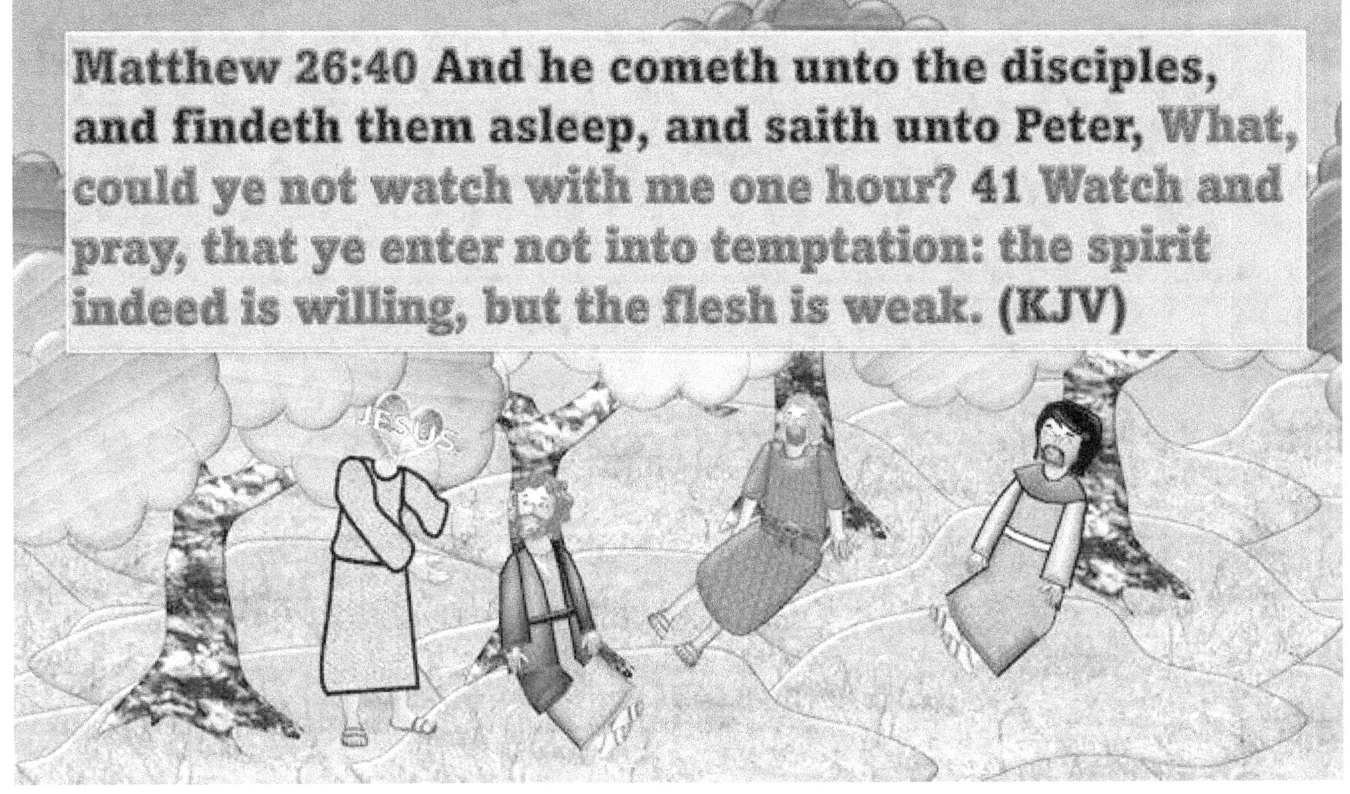

BIBLE CLUES (KJV) — Examine 4 Gospels for Clues (KJV)

Matthew 26:42	Mark 14:39	Luke	John 17:6-19
42 He went away again the second time, and prayed, saying, **O my Father, if this cup may not pass away from me, except I drink it, thy will be done.**	**39** And again he went away, and prayed, and spake the same words.	He references the third prayer only.	**JESUS PRAYS FOR HIS DISCIPLES** **6** I have manifested thy name unto the men which thou gavest me out of the world: thine they were, and thou gavest them me; and they have kept thy word. **7** Now they have known that all things whatsoever thou hast given me are of thee. **8** For I have given unto them the words which thou gavest me; and they have received them, and have known surely that I came out from thee, and they have believed that thou didst send me. **9** I pray for them: I pray not for the world, but for them which thou hast given me; for they are thine. **10** And all mine are thine, and thine are mine; and I am glorified in them. **11** And now I am no more in the world, but these are in the world, and I come to thee. Holy Father, keep through thine own name those whom thou hast given me, that they may be one, as we are. **12** While I was with them in the world, I kept them in thy name: those that thou gavest me I have kept, and none of them is lost, but the son of perdition; that the scripture might be fulfilled. (PRAYER CONTINUED) ⟶

John 17:13-19 JESUS PRAYS FOR HIS DISCIPLES continued

13 And now come I to thee; and these things I speak in the world, that they might have my joy fulfilled in themselves. I have given them thy word; and the world hath hated them, because they are not of the world, even as I am not of the world.

15 I pray not that thou shouldest take them out of the world, but that thou shouldest keep them from the evil. **16** They are not of the world, even as I am not of the world. **17** Sanctify them through thy truth: thy word is truth.

18 As thou hast sent me into the world, even so have I also sent them into the world. **19** And for their sakes I sanctify myself, that they also might be sanctified through the truth.

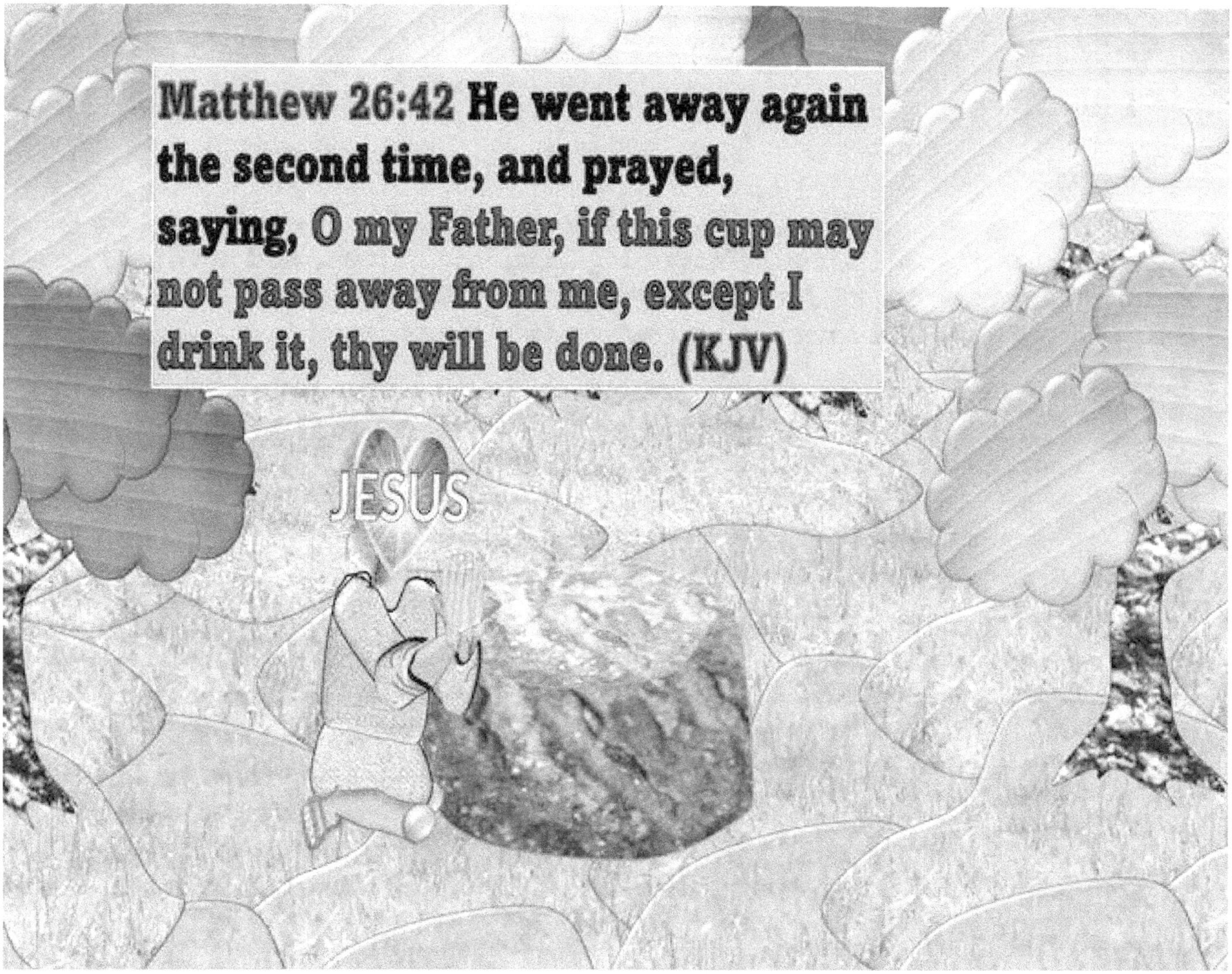

Another challenge Jesus faced was the loss of the fulfilling friendships He had formed with His twelve Disciples. Yes, Judas turned away. And yes, He knew that due to Peter's fear, He would turn away but later return with greater zeal. Knowing that all of the remaining eleven Disciples, including Peter, would scatter, leaving Him alone and stranded had to hurt.

From a human standpoint, experiencing a mother's love had been fantastic. Learning carpentry at the knees of His foster father, Joseph, had been a delight. Experiencing life as a human had its ups and downs, of course. But most of it was full of rewards.

Jesus had reveled in bringing healing to so many people. It had been fun to travel with twelve close-knit friends. He was going to miss so many things about this earthly life. Naturally, there were several aspects He would not miss; nevertheless, it had been a satisfying experience.

All He and His Father had ever wanted was a family of men, women, and children with whom they enjoyed solid relationships. Almighty God had created Adam and Eve to fill that need, but they rejected that opportunity.

Moses had been the closest Jesus had to an ongoing friendship during those forty years of the Exodus. It had been a delight to continue that friendship once Moses reached Heaven. It was also reassuring to receive His counsel when Moses and Elijah came for a brief visit forty days before He was crucified.

Jesus, in Luke 9:28, ... took Peter and John and James, and went up into a mountain to pray. 29 And as he prayed, the fashion of his countenance was altered, and his raiment was white and glistering.

Luke 9:30 And, behold, there talked with him two men, which were Moses and Elias (i.e., Elijah): 31 Who appeared in glory, and spake of his decease which he should accomplish at Jerusalem. (KJV)

Years later, Peter wrote, in 2 Peter 1:16 For we did not follow cleverly devised stories when we told you about the coming of our Lord Jesus Christ in power, but we were eyewitnesses of his majesty.

2 Peter 1:17 He received honor and glory from God the Father when the voice came to him from the Majestic Glory, saying, "This is my Son, whom I love; with him I am well pleased." 18 We ourselves heard this voice that came from heaven when we were with him on the sacred mountain. (KJV)

Jesus did take comfort in the picture the Holy Spirit placed in His mind of future friendships/relationships with Christians such as you and I and other faithful followers of Christ. He especially relished the realization that there would be those who would not just come to Him in petition for healing or answers; there would also be those who loved to spend time with Him by reading the WORD of the Holy Bible or who honestly loved spending time with Him in Communion or Prayer or even ongoing conversations. That brought true solace to His **L**oving (with a capital **L**) Heart.

But the part that Jesus might have felt to be even more painful than the upcoming physical torture would be due to the following few facts:

1 To save all humankind, Jesus was going to have to become a boiling mass of sin. He would have to absorb into His body, a body that never had sinned, millions upon millions of sins of every sort.

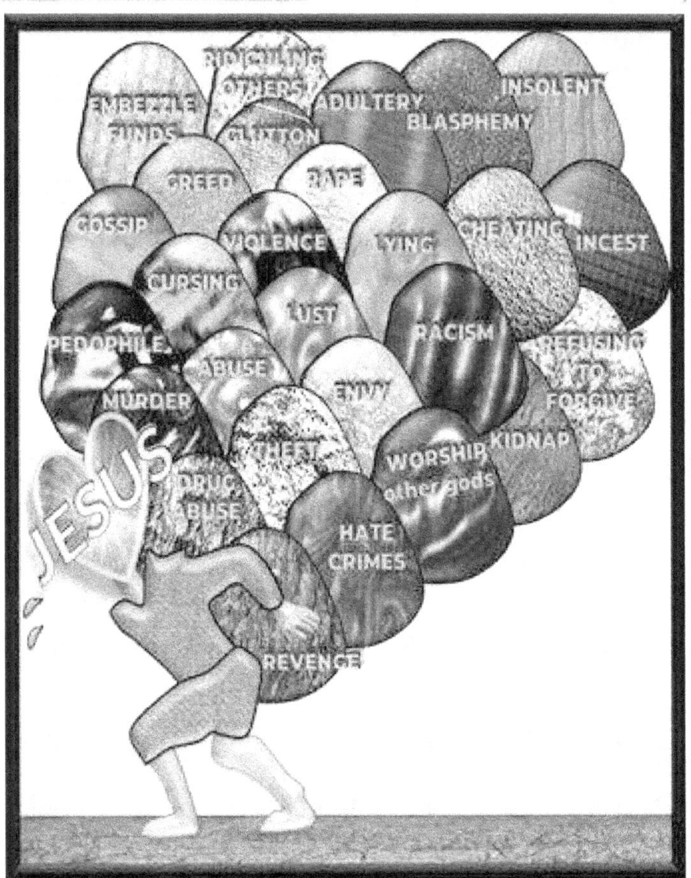

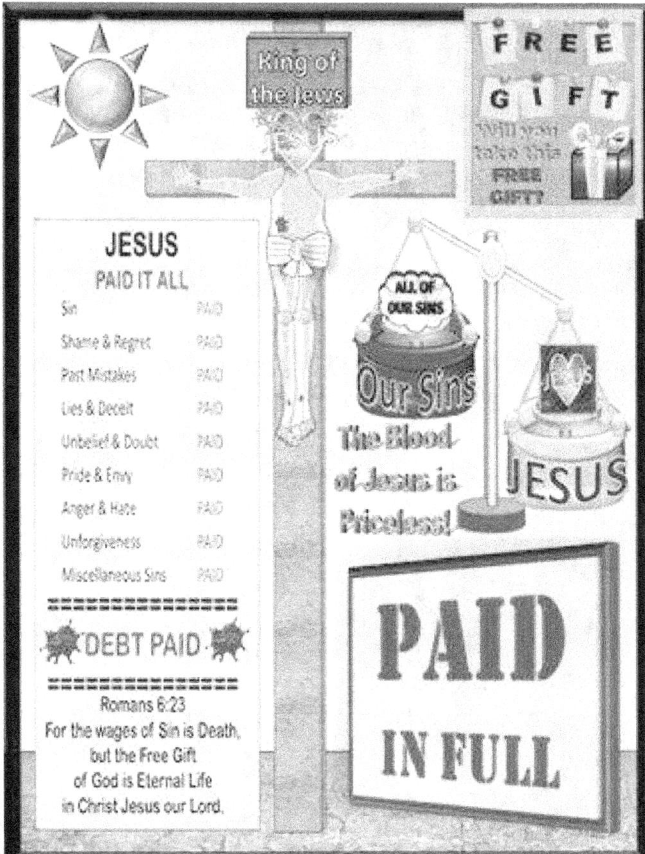

2 Jesus had never even thrown a tantrum as a child, as He couldn't bear the thought of hurting or disappointing His beautiful, loving mother. He was never disrespectful to His foster father, Joseph, as He was aware of what an extreme sacrifice Joseph had made to keep His mother and Him safe and protected from Herod's far-reaching murderous hand. But now, during the up to six hours He would hang on the cross, in silence, He would have to experience, up close and personal, every single sin, large and small, committed by every single human who had ever walked the planet, was currently walking the planet, and who would walk the planet in the future.

Jesus would even have to experience the sins that made some of the Recording Angels blanch or tremble, such as pedophiles, sex traffickers, and priests harming children in a sexual way or overzealous enslavers, schoolmasters, or parents who beat their charges / students / children unmercifully or sacrificed them to false gods.

Nevertheless, Jesus was willing to do this to save humankind from hell.

3 More challenging would be when He would have to endure being cut off from His ongoing unity with His Heavenly Father. Never once, in all of millennia, had He ever been solo as an I. It had always been a WE as Father God, Holy Spirit, and Jesus. They had always been the Triune God. He had been in constant communication with both of them every day during His time on earth. Every lesson He had ever taught was first downloaded to Him from Above.

> **John 14:10** Believest thou not that I am in the Father, and the Father in me? the words that I speak unto you I speak not of myself: but the Father that dwelleth in me, he doeth the works.
>
> **John 5:19 Then answered Jesus and said unto them,** Verily, verily, I say unto you, The Son can do nothing of himself, but what he seeth the Father do: for what things soever he doeth, these also doeth the Son likewise. (KJV)

You may wonder why Almighty God needed to turn His back on His only Begotten Son. To my understanding, Father God could not soil Himself with sin. Otherwise, He would no longer be perfect and true. Jesus could get His hands dirty. The Holy Spirit was also able to withstand the stain of our sins. But God the Father must remain and stay sin-free.

That is also part of why they cannot permit any sinful person to become a resident of Heaven. We have to be covered by the Blood of Christ, or we must go to the only other place that exists for the dead to inhabit: Hades/hell.

I imagine that being cut off from His Father, even for just 1 to 3 days, might be how we might feel to have a limb amputated or an eye removed.

> **1 John 4:14 And we have seen and do testify that the Father sent the Son to be** the Saviour of the world. (KJV)
>
> **Romans 5:8 But God commendeth his love toward us, in that, while we were yet sinners,** Christ died for us. (KJV)
>
> **Hebrews 4:15 For we do not have a high priest who is unable to empathize with our weaknesses, but we have one who has been tempted in every way, just as we are--yet** he did not sin. (NIV)

Second time Jesus found trio sleeping.

BIBLE CLUES — Examine 4 Gospels for Clues (KJV) — BIBLE CLUES		
Matthew 26:43	**Mark 14:40**	**Luke & John**
43 And he came and found them asleep again: for their eyes were heavy.	40 And when he returned, he found them asleep again, (for their eyes were heavy,) neither wist they what to answer him.	No Reference to this Topic.

Jesus must have been extraordinarily lonely when He found His Disciples sleeping; men who claimed to lay down their lives for Him, could not stay awake during His painful vigil. He was already facing abandonment issues with His Father and the Holy Spirit. Now, in advance, He was facing the fact that no human comfort was available to Him.

In desperation, when Jesus awakened them to question why they could not stay awake, neither Peter, John, nor James could devise any believable excuse. That may have been the tipping point to catapult Jesus into deep grief.

Jesus' 3rd of 3 Prayers for Strength

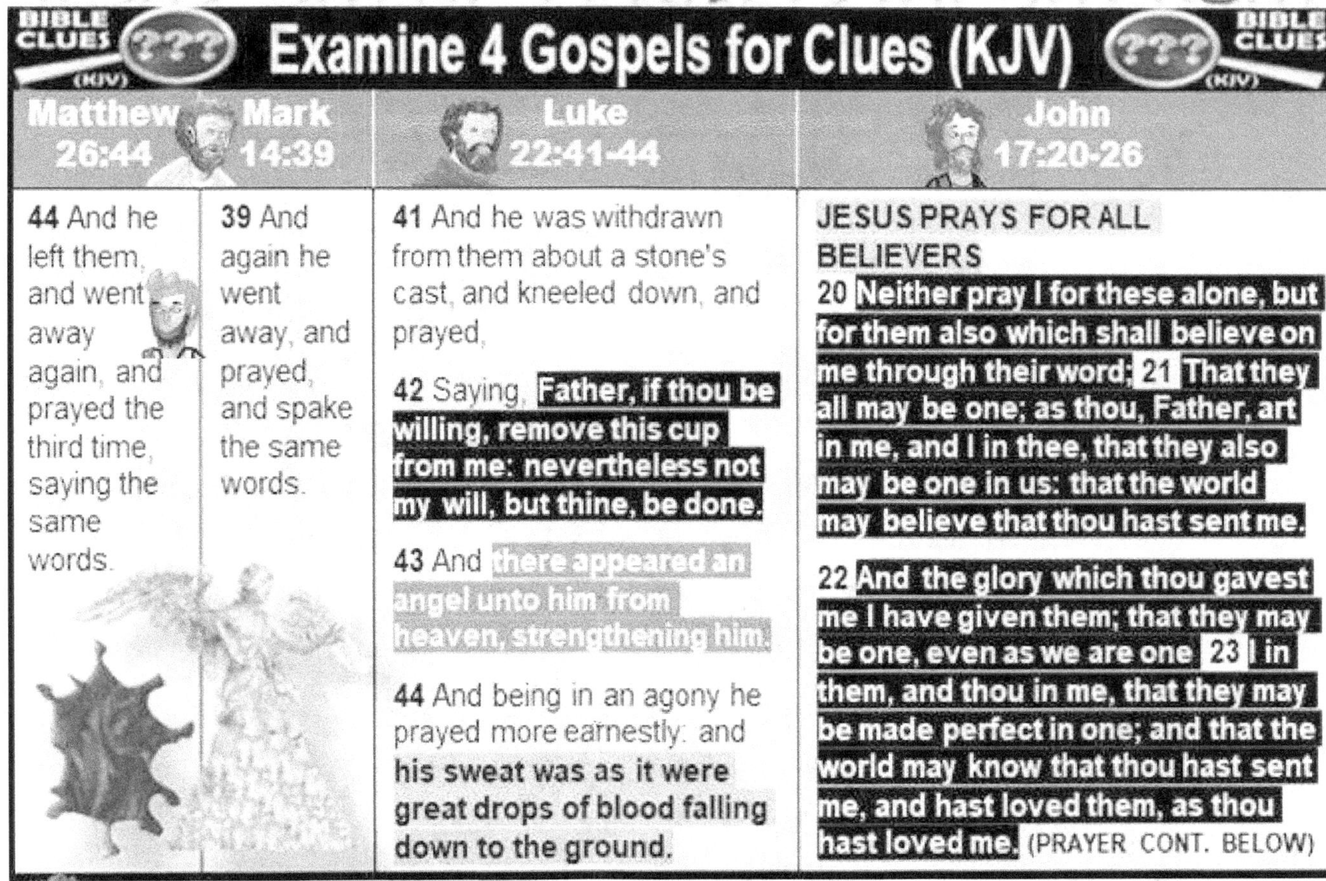

Matthew 26:44	Mark 14:39	Luke 22:41-44	John 17:20-26
44 And he left them, and went away again, and prayed the third time, saying the same words.	**39** And again he went away, and prayed, and spake the same words.	**41** And he was withdrawn from them about a stone's cast, and kneeled down, and prayed, **42** Saying, Father, if thou be willing, remove this cup from me: nevertheless not my will, but thine, be done. **43** And there appeared an angel unto him from heaven, strengthening him. **44** And being in an agony he prayed more earnestly: and his sweat was as it were great drops of blood falling down to the ground.	JESUS PRAYS FOR ALL BELIEVERS **20** Neither pray I for these alone, but for them also which shall believe on me through their word: **21** That they all may be one; as thou, Father, art in me, and I in thee, that they also may be one in us: that the world may believe that thou hast sent me. **22** And the glory which thou gavest me I have given them; that they may be one, even as we are one **23** I in them, and thou in me, that they may be made perfect in one; and that the world may know that thou hast sent me, and hast loved them, as thou hast loved me. (PRAYER CONT. BELOW)

John 17:24-26 JESUS PRAYS FOR ALL BELIEVERS continued

24 Father, I will that they also, whom thou hast given me, be with me where I am; that they may behold my glory, which thou hast given me: for thou lovedst me before the foundation of the world.

25 O righteous Father, the world hath not known thee: but I have known thee, and these have known that thou hast sent me.

26 And I have declared unto them thy name, and will declare it: that the love wherewith thou hast loved me may be in them, and I in them.

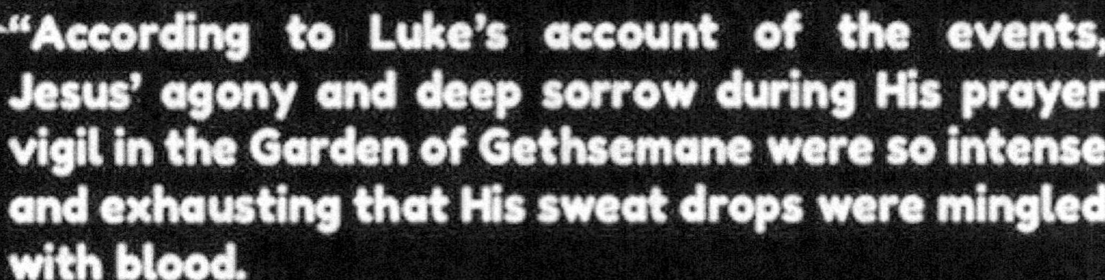

"According to Luke's account of the events, Jesus' agony and deep sorrow during His prayer vigil in the Garden of Gethsemane were so intense and exhausting that His sweat drops were mingled with blood.

Luke, who was a physician, was describing an actual medical condition called Hematohidrosis in which a person literally sweats drops of blood.

This rare condition can stem from various causes, including high stress and excessive exertion, causing the person's blood to press through the membrane of the blood vessels and penetrate through the skin.

No one can ever imagine the pressure, stress, and agony that Jesus experienced during His prayer time on that night so long ago at Gethsemane."

> **Luke 22:41 And he was withdrawn from them about a stone's cast, and kneeled down, and prayed,**
>
> **Luke 22:42 Saying, Father, if thou be willing, remove this cup from me: nevertheless not my will, but thine, be done.**
>
> **Luke 22:43 And there appeared an angel unto him from heaven, strengthening him.**
>
> **Luke 22:44 And being in an agony he prayed more earnestly: and his sweat was as it were great drops of blood falling down to the ground.** [KJV]

For the third time, Jesus plodded away to His prayer arena, feeling greater agony than He had ever felt in His earthly life. In despair, He threw Himself down. On his knees, He pleaded, "**Father, I know this is the third time I am asking this of You, but please, ..., please, ..., please consider carefully. Father, if thou be willing, remove this cup from me: nevertheless not my will, but thine, be done.**" [Luke 22:42]

It must have been extraordinarily tough to yield total control like that to His Father. This meant that should the answer be "NO," which Jesus already knew would be "NO," and had to be "NO," then this meant that He would have to endure perhaps the most excruciating pain any man, woman, or child would ever have to endure. For it was not just the physical pain He would be facing, which was almost unspeakable in how tormentingly painful it would be; Jesus was also going to have His very insides taking in and absorbing every sin devised by the evil imagination of Satan and enacted by humankind. To top it off, His Father and the Holy Spirit would have to willingly turn their back on Jesus for all the hours He hung on the Cross. To save humankind from the perils of hell, the other two-thirds of the Triune God must not be accessories to the crimes and sins and *'missing of the marks'* perpetuated by me, by you, and by all humankind from the past, present, and future. If Father God and the Holy Spirit acknowledged Jesus during that stretch of time, they would be enablers instead of deniers of our human sin-natures. For the best interests of all humankind, they must turn their backs on the one they LOVE the most.

Abruptly, the human side of Him overrode His divine nature as He cried out, **Father, ..., I am petrified! I am so scared. By the time they get through with me, I am going to look like a shredded piece of meat and barely human. How am I supposed to withstand this unbearable pain? Please, help me be strong enough to go through with this! Abba! Abbaaaaaa!!!**"

In my imagination, I can picture the Angels of Heaven pacing back and forth in agony, longing to be allowed to offer comfort in some manner. I also imagine Father God and the Holy Spirit having large tears pouring from their visage.

In the 2017 movie, 'The Shack,' it felt authentic that the actors playing the part of God and the Holy Spirit had scars on their wrists. That felt soul-satisfying that even though two-thirds of the Triune God were forced, for the sake of humankind, to turn their back on Jesus, their 'comrade in arms,' they were, in reality, as close as they could be as they, too, suffered right along with Jesus.

I think that Almighty God chose the most maternal or the most benevolent of all the Angels to swoop down to the Garden of Gethsemane to bring as much comfort as possible. It might have been an Archangel such as Gabriel or Michael. It might have been a female or male Angel with whom Jesus felt the strongest bond. This Angel probably took Jesus into his or her arms as He cried harder than He had ever cried before.

FYI - In America, we have the term **ugly cried** *to indicate that Jesus, like a terrified child, was likely blubbering, bawling, whimpering, sniveling, wailing, and groaning. It would not have been a pretty sight nor pleasant to listen to. I think that this Angel, utilizing the wisdom of the Holy Spirit, was aware that not one word should be proffered during those moments. Instead, the Angel tenderly held Jesus in his or her arms and allowed Him to get this out of His system as much as possible.*

We know that Jesus was so agonized and petrified with fear that His sweat was a mixture of normal sweat and blood.

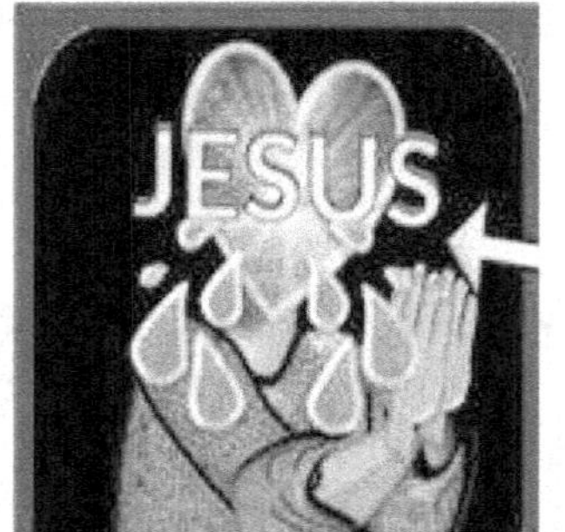

If we are ever tempted to downplay or deny how much Jesus LOVES us beyond any Love we have ever felt by those around us, this is what we should consider. We should picture His prayers in the garden. We should recall that He had to withstand the Romans whipping Him 39 or 40 times. We should remind ourselves that Jesus allowed the Roman soldiers to nail Him to the Cross for our sake. He was so eager to save us from going to hell that Jesus even willingly paid the price for all the sins any of us had ever sinned, are currently sinning, and will sin in the future. That is a Love that not one of us deserves or is worthy of; nevertheless, Jesus Loved us that much anyway. Equal to that Love is the Love felt by God the Father and the Holy Spirit who allowed Jesus to suffer unspeakably for our sakes. The Triune God Loves us with more Love than we can imagine. I don't know about you. As for me, I feel like I owe them everything! God Loves a cheerful giver. I cheerfully dedicate the rest of my days, weeks, months, and years, however many or few they may be, to willingly serve the Triune God!

Here is a 2022 hymn written by Jeremy Riddle that represents this act of Love better than any hymn I have ever been blessed to hear. It is called **'We Crown You.'** I urge you to listen to it on YouTube, with or without lyrics. See the links:

Riddle, Jeremy on YouTube. (February 2024). WE CROWN YOU – LIVE IN THE PRAYER ROOM | JEREMY RIDDLE. Website: https://www.youtube.com/watch?v=tsLKnyDrDBE

Water in the Desert on YouTube. (February 2024). We Crown You - Jeremy Riddle (Lyrics). Website: https://www.youtube.com/watch?v=UKyWlh9GiTc

Eventually, Jesus managed to calm down. Then, I imagine Father God said, ""

I picture Jesus pulling away from the arms of His Angel, straightening His posture, and listening intently. Thankfully, due to His Triune nature, they could communicate telepathically, infinitely faster than I would need to type these words on my laptop.

It was a good thing, too, as Jesus would have already been aware of hundreds of lost sheep, including Judas Iscariot, some power-hungry Pharisees, and 300 to 600 Sanhedrin soldiers, at the foot of the Mount of Olives, stealthily and steadily marching in their direction.

I imagine that Jesus felt filled with compassionate Love for each of them and all the rest of us who had ever walked or would ever walk the earth. I am confident that Jesus would gather us under His protective wing, if He could, to prevent us from falling into that dark abyss.

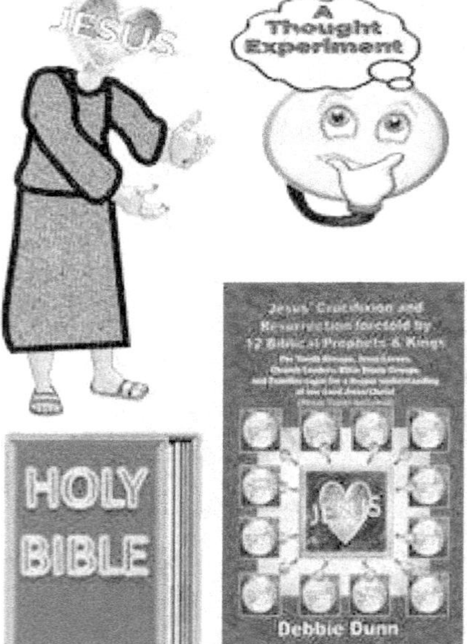

I imagine Jesus might have thought the following things:

"In addition to the Holy Bible, it is vital that people have the opportunity to view movies, read Biblical reenactment books, recall Bible stories, analyze what is stated and interpreted by Biblical scholars, hear sermons, listen to Christian videos and concerts, and sing songs that demonstrate how deeply Loved each of you are by the . As for this book, it was written to alert you to what is at stake regarding your Salvation. This book, and others like it, are written for you, your loved ones, the companions of your heart, and for people of all colors, all races, and all religious (or lack thereof) persuasions. No one exists outside of my Love. It does not matter what you have done or haven't done. I fully LOVE you all!"

I understand that the Triune God, who lives outside of TIME, could look at what had already happened, what was currently happening, and what would one day happen and witness it all happening simultaneously. As Jesus' far-reaching gaze rested upon those of us still alive in 2024, and beyond, He saw how people were playing right into Satan's hands.

You only have to see what is happening in the world to be aware that the time of Tribulation, described in the book of Revelation, is not far off. Satan is well aware that He loses in the end; however, he is determined to drag as many people as he can into hell right along with him. He may pretend to love and admire you. He may even bribe you with money, fame, or other enticing gifts. In reality, he hates all of us humans whom God universally loves. Are any of you willingly making a covenant with Satan, thus making it easy for him or his minions to entrap you? Please, reconsider!

Matthew 6:24 "No one can serve two masters; for either he will hate the one and love the other, or he will be devoted to the one and despise the other. You cannot serve God and mammon [money, possessions, fame, status, or whatever is valued more than the Lord]." (AMPLIFIED BIBLE)

Jesus realized that the one and only way to save us from that horrible fate, an eternity spent in the Lake of Fire. He had to continue walking this path. He had known it from before He served His time on earth. It was simply the human side of Him that hoped there might be some clever reprieve to bypass the excruciating pain He would have to suffer. But since that was not the case, His love for us far exceeded His fear.

Jesus might have proclaimed words such as this. "Father, I will follow through on this unspeakable path to save those who languish in prison cells; those who have lost loved ones to vengeful others; those who feel lonely, unworthy of love, or isolated; those who deal with persecution for My sake; those who endure war, acts of terrorism, or hate crimes; and those who struggle to lead righteous lives. I love each of them collectively and individually. So, yes, I will drink this bitter cup. Please grace me with the courage to endure until the end."

These Bible verses describe part of what Jesus hoped to save us from.

1 John 3:7 Dear children, do not let anyone lead you astray. The one who does what is right is righteous, just as he is righteous. 8 The one who does what is sinful is of the devil, because the devil has been sinning from the beginning. The reason the Son of God appeared was to destroy the devil's work. (NIV)

James 4:7 Submit yourselves, then, to God. Resist the devil, and he will flee from you. 8 Come near to God and he will come near to you. Wash your hands, you sinners, and purify your hearts, you double-minded. ... 10 Humble yourselves before the Lord, and he will lift you up. (NIV)

Hebrews 9:22 In fact, the law requires that nearly everything be cleansed with blood, and without the shedding of blood there is no forgiveness. (NIV)

There were just a few short minutes left before Judas and hundreds of arresting officers would arrive. As Jesus struggled to rise, His legs might have felt wobbly. The angel probably reached out a helping hand. Filled with compassion, the angelic being likely gave Jesus one last comforting hug. As they pulled apart, the angel ignored the bloodstains on his (or her) robe. It might even become a treasured possession up in Heaven. For a brief second, Jesus might have felt tempted to follow that angel to His Celestial home. But then, He reminded Himself what was at stake: The salvation of all humankind.

Jesus knew full well that the Recording Angels had been documenting every good and evil thought, word-statements, or deed perpetuated by every human being from Adam and Eve forward. They even calculated what sins the humans, not yet born, including you and me, would potentially perpetuate during their/our lifetimes.

Ecclesiastes 12:14 For God shall bring every work into judgment, with every secret thing, whether it be good, or whether it be evil. (KJV)

2 Corinthians 5:10 For we must all appear before the judgment seat of Christ; that every one may receive the things done in his body, according to that he hath done, whether it be good or bad. (KJV)

Revelation 20:12 And I saw the dead, small and great, stand before God; and the books were opened: and another book was opened, which is the book of life: and the dead were judged out of those things which were written in the books, according to their works. (KJV)

If you grew up in America from 1934 forward, you might not find it strange to consider that some invisible being watches you while you are awake or asleep, recording your good and bad deeds. Consider the lighthearted Christmas Carol called 'Santa Claus is Comin' to Town.' Take note of three of these verses, in particular, in the following image.

> **Luke 8:17** For nothing is secret, that shall not be made manifest; neither any thing hid, that shall not be known and come abroad. **(KJV)**

On a more serious note, Santa Claus and the Heavenly Recording Angels are not the only ones vigilantly watching and recording every word we say and every deed we act upon. Either Satan himself or one or more of his minions is keeping a watchful eye on the ways they can get a legal hold on us. They want to try to interfere in our walk with Christ in every way they can. They take great pleasure in lying to us that to act on a fleshly desire will be no big deal and are quickly forgiven by the all-forgiving Christ. But then, as soon as we give into that desire, they will pollute our ears with all manner of accusations of how we don't deserve the name of Christian as we followed their advice to miss the mark by sinning.

Satan and his minions want to distract us from the fact that our Salvation has little to do with our works but everything to do with what Christ sacrificed for us on the Cross. By the Triune God's grace, He accepts us into the Body of Christ as long as we sincerely:

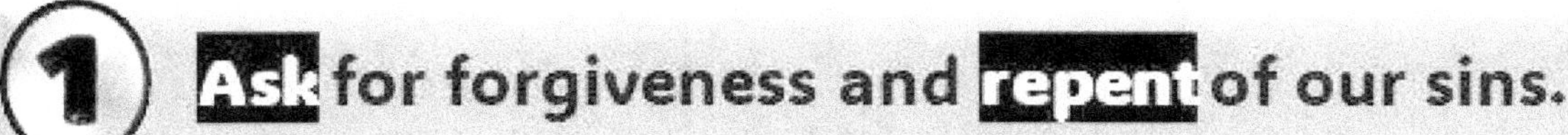

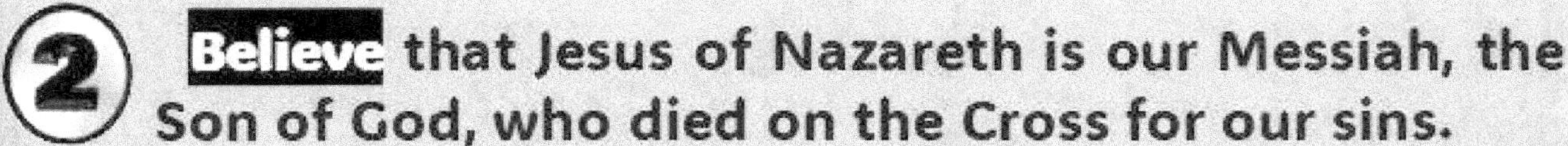

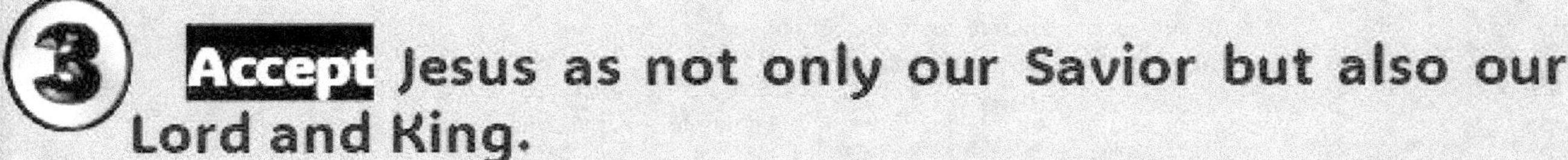

To illustrate, check out the following nine (9) illustrations..

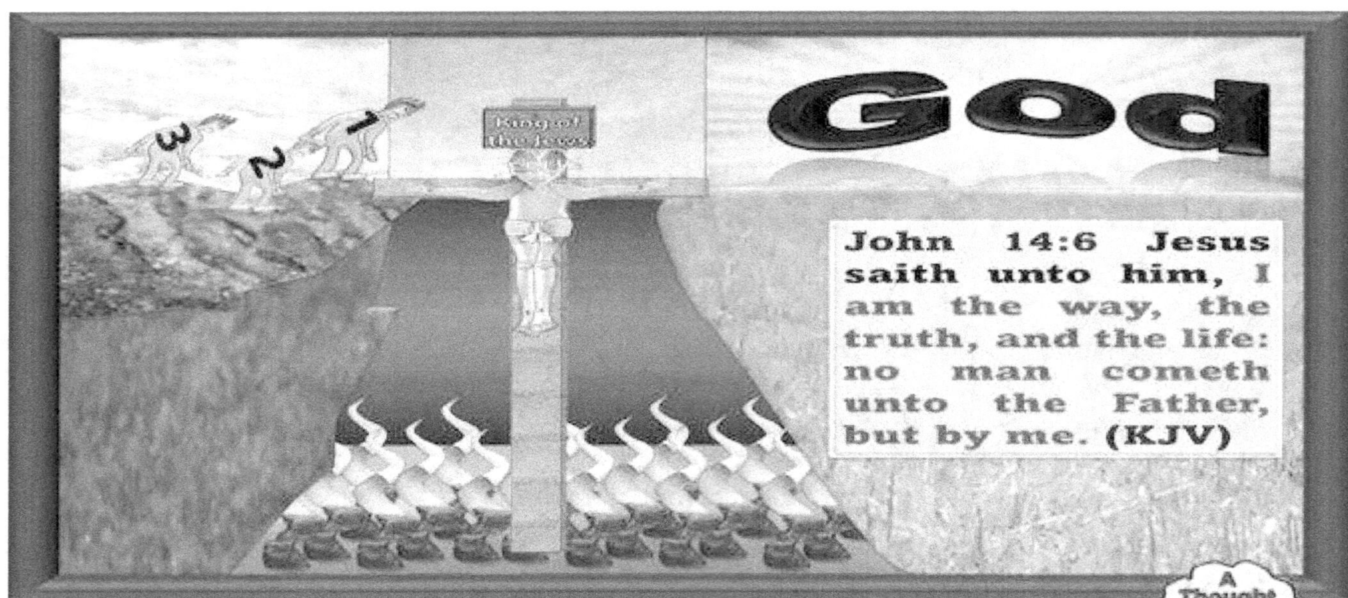

Imagine three **unsaved** individuals die and reach Heaven's realm. The guy in front will be the first to be judged. The guy in the middle will be the second to be judged. The guy in back will be the third to be judged. The **Holy Spirit** will instruct and question each man. Afterward, **Jesus** will determine if that particular individual will be eligible to enter Heaven for his new forever home.

2

HOLY SPIRIT

God

John 14:6 Jesus saith unto him, I am the way, the truth, and the life: no man cometh unto the Father, but by me. (KJV)

The bill for all your sins has already been paid when our Lord Jesus died on the cross. As long as you repent, you will be forgiven. Do you repent?

Wow! I never knew that. I have been sorry for a long time. So, yes, I repent.

1

I am gonna lie, but I'm not sorry!

2

3

Yeah, what he said. I'm sorry, too.

3

HOLY SPIRIT

God

John 14:6 Jesus saith unto him, I am the way, the truth, and the life: no man cometh unto the Father, but by me. (KJV)

In Heaven, all thoughts can be heard, and your heart can be read. Since you are no longer eligible for Heaven, hell is your only destination. We feel great sorrow!

Nooooooo! Ahhhhh!

3

1

2

A Thought Experiment

4
HOLY SPIRIT
God
John 14:6 Jesus saith unto him, I am the way, the truth, and the life: no man cometh unto the Father, but by me. (KJV)
Do you believe that Jesus is the Messiah and that His Love for you was so great that He was willing to be tortured and die on a cross to save all of humankind?
Gulp! I don't know why I'm crying. No one ever explained it to me that way. That's amazing! Thank you, Jesus! Yes, I believe it, but I'm sorry for your pain!
Yeah, what he said. I believe, too!
1
2
A Thought Experiment

5
HOLY SPIRIT
God
John 14:6 Jesus saith unto him, I am the way, the truth, and the life: no man cometh unto the Father, but by me. (KJV)
Here is the last question. Do you accept Jesus as your Savior, your Lord, and your King?
Yes! I never understood any of this until now. But now that I do, I am willing and happy to serve you as my Savior, my Lord, and my King. King Jesus, thank you for giving me this second chance!
1
2

6

HOLY SPIRIT

God
JESUS

John 14:6 Jesus saith unto him, I am the way, the truth, and the life: no man cometh unto the Father, but by me. (KJV)

Well done! Well done! Welcome Home! We are all so happy to have you join us here in Heaven for your new FOREVER HOME! An Angel will now give you the grand tour.

1

2

A bunch of angels started singing in celebration. Jesus jumped onto the bridge to welcome him. The Angel guard blocked the path of the other man while everyone else's focus was on welcoming the new resident into Heaven.

A Thought Experiment

7

HOLY SPIRIT

God

John 14:6 Jesus saith unto him, I am the way, the truth, and the life: no man cometh unto the Father, but by me. (KJV)

It is your turn now. You must answer for yourself and not use another man's words. For your final question, do you sincerely accept Jesus as your Savior, your Lord, and your King?

2

Well, um, ..., well, I can buy into that Jesus saved us. So, yes, I can accept Him as my Savior. But I live in the U.S.A. We don't have no kings. He could be my President. But I can't bow to him like He was my King. Sorry. I just can't do that!

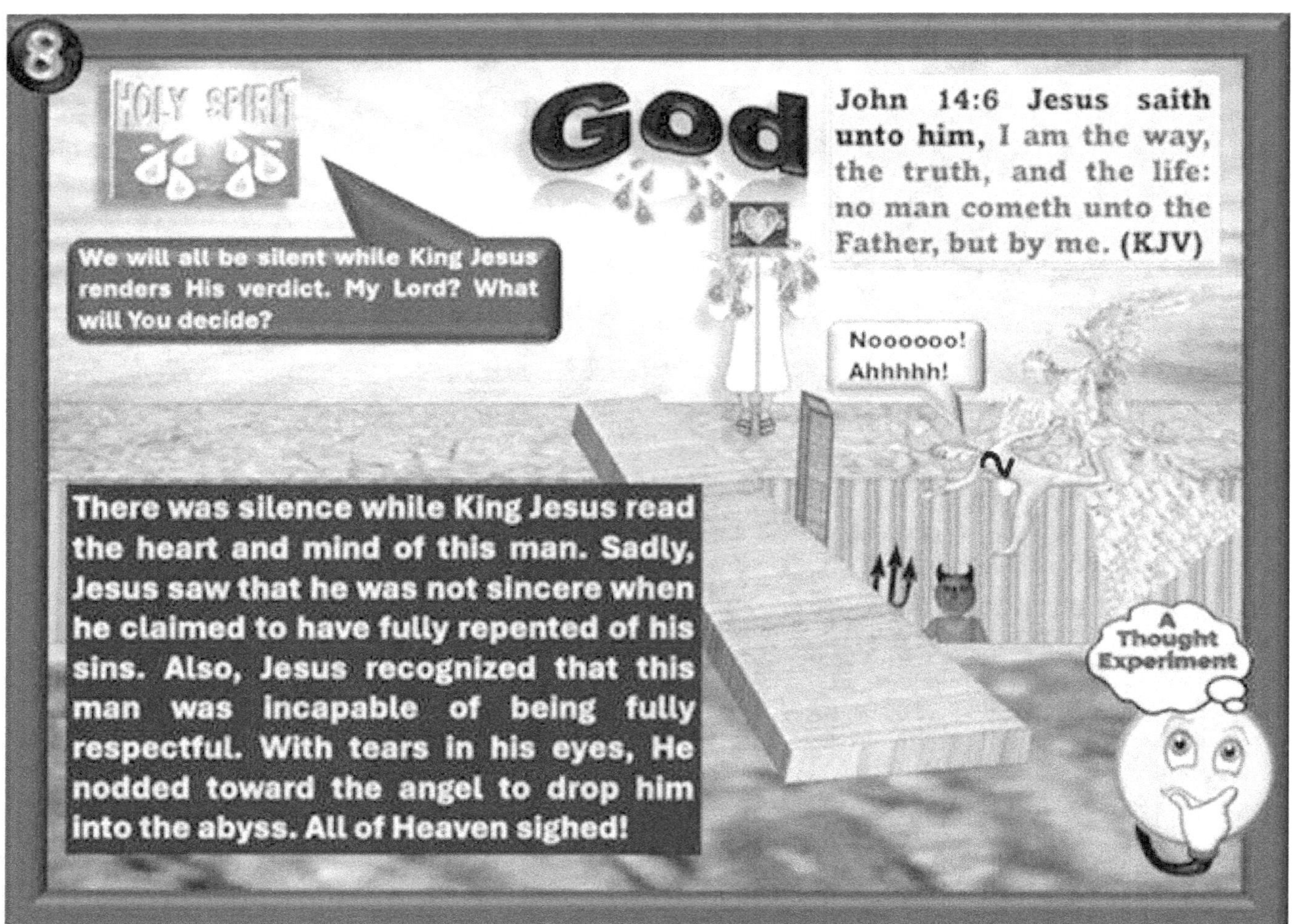

In the above scenario, if you died as a Saved Christian, you would arrive directly in the Third Heaven. You would not have to cross that proverbial bridge. Since the Blood of Jesus will already cover you, it will be as if you never sinned. See the confirmation of this in these Bible verses.

Luke 15:10 **Likewise, I say unto you, there is joy in the presence of the angels of God over one sinner who repents.** (KJV)

Hebrews 8:12 **For I will be merciful to their unrighteousness, and their sins and their iniquities will I remember no more.** (KJV)

Jeremiah 31:34 **And they shall teach no more every man his neighbour, and every man his brother, saying, Know the Lord: for they shall all know me, from the least of them unto the greatest of them, saith the Lord: for I will forgive their iniquity, and I will remember their sin no more.** (KJV)

Isaiah 43:25 **I, even I, am He that blots out your transgressions for mine own sake, and will not remember your sins.** (KJV)

Timothy 2:5 **For there is one God, and one mediator between God and men, the man Christ Jesus; 6 Who gave himself a ransom for all, to be testified in due time.** (KJV)

Internally reminded of this, Jesus walked with new resolve toward His sleeping Disciples and His preordained fate.

> **John 15:13 Greater love hath no man than this, that a man lay down his life for his friends. (KJV)**

Third time Jesus found trio sleeping.

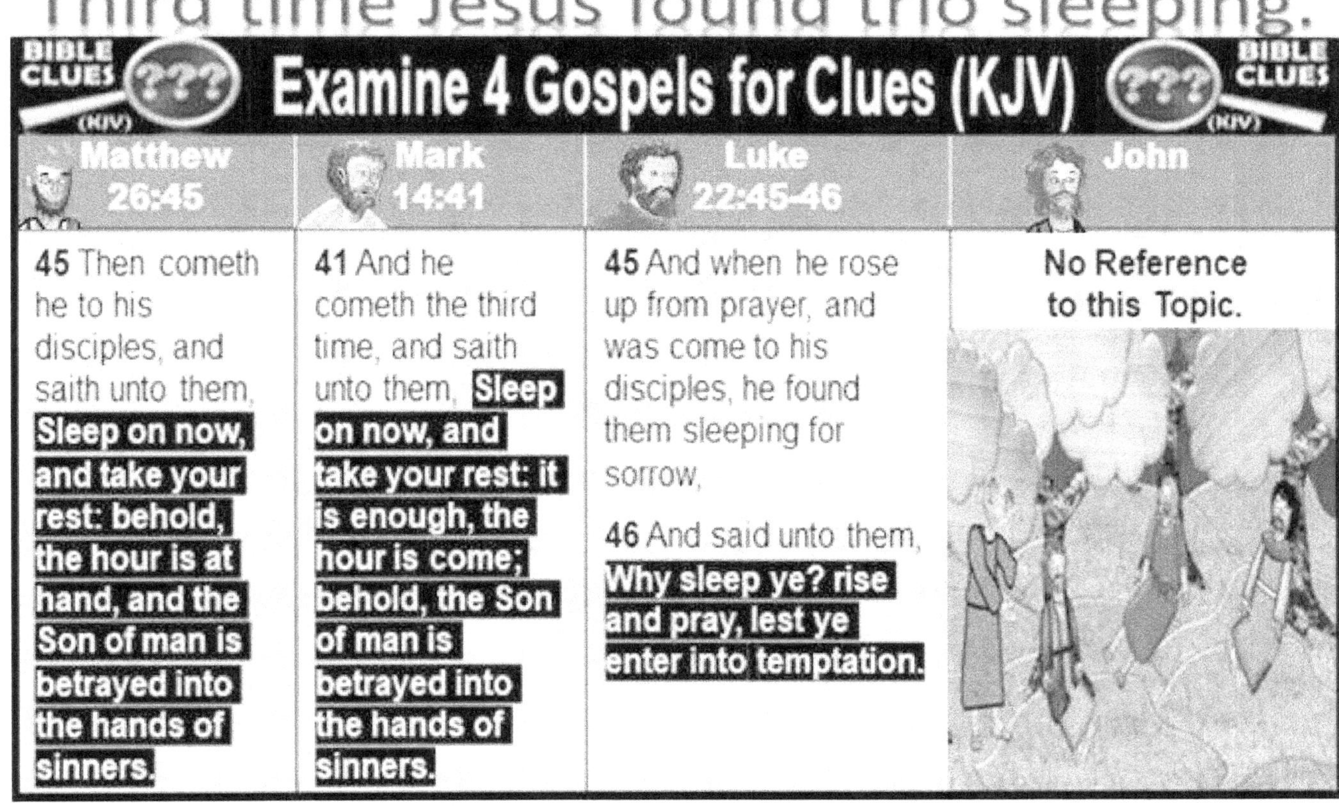

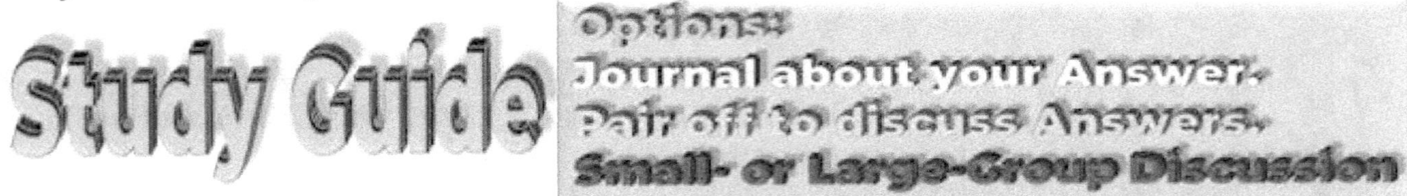

1. That Thursday night, Jesus and the eleven remaining Disciples divided into three groups. Group 1 comprised eight men: Andrew, Bartholomew, Matthew, Simon the Zealot, Thaddaeus, Thomas, Philip, and Little James. Group 2 included three men: Big James Z., John Z., and Peter. Group 3 was made up of Jesus praying to His Heavenly Father.

    A. Describe what you think happened with the eight men in Group 1.

    B. Describe why Jesus' favorite Disciples, from Group 2, could not stay awake as requested. What was going on with them?

    C. Describe what you think was going through Jesus' mind. What was the content of His prayers?

2. Explain why you think Jesus was sweating blood while He prayed.

3. Even though Jesus was born knowing that He was to be the sacrificial Lamb who would save all humankind, what are your thoughts about why He begged His Father to change that plan at the last moment?

4. What do you think would have happened to us if God had agreed to prevent the crucifixion from happening?

5. Why do you think it was important that Jesus had never sinned even once?

6. If our Heavenly Father chose you to be the angel who came down to comfort Jesus while He was praying, what do you think you could have done to comfort Him?

7. Let's imagine that you are the Holy Spirit. Jesus needs you to remind Him of all the reasons why He must go through with the plan to allow Himself to be arrested, tortured, and crucified. He wants you to list all the ways humankind will benefit if He follows through with this plan.

8. As the Holy Spirit, describe all the ways humankind would suffer if Jesus did not go through with this plan.

9. Why do you believe Jesus agreed to have this happen to Him?

10. Imagine you look up and suddenly see Jesus standing right in front of you. Describe to Him how His sacrifice benefited your life and the lives of people around the world. What else would you like to say to Him?

THIRTY PIECES OF SILVER

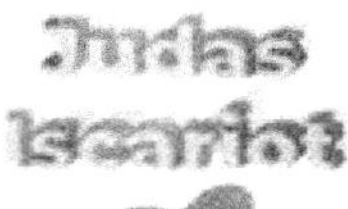

Jesus chose the Disciple best at math, Judas Iscariot, as their Treasurer. Sadly, per **John 12:6**, "he was a thief; as keeper of the money bag, he used to help himself to what was put into it."

A group of elite priests and elders called the Sanhedrin wanted to arrest the popular Jesus from Galilee. They needed an inside man. But who?

Luke (**Luke 22:3**) and John (**John 13:2**) said Satan or the Devil entered Judas' heart. On the day that came to be known as 'Spy Wednesday,' Judas secretly went to the Jerusalem Temple. He met with the powerful and wealthy Sadducees. Their Chief Priest convinced Judas to betray his master for the least amount he could offer: 30 pieces of silver.

FYI - Thirty pieces of silver were not worth much in those days. Let's say you owned an ox who gored somebody's servant to death. Read the Bible verse below to see how much money you must compensate their master.

Exodus 21:32 If the ox shall push a manservant or a maidservant; he shall give unto their master thirty shekels of silver and the ox shall be stoned. (KJV)

Matthew 26:14 Then one of the twelve, called Judas Iscariot, went unto the chief priests, 15 And said unto them, What will ye give me, and I will deliver him unto you? And they covenanted with him for thirty pieces of silver.

Matthew 26:16 And from that time he sought opportunity to betray him. (KJV)

Psalm 109, written by King David, became known as the Judas or Iscariot Psalm. Why?

In the verses, King David described himself as a man of prayer. His wicked former friend betrayed him with **evil words of hatred** and a **lying tongue**.

In **Psalm 109:5**, David complained, "They repay me evil for good, and hatred for my friendship." (KJV)

Why did Judas betray Jesus?

Jesus treated Judas with courtesy and love. He trusted him so much that He allowed Judas to be the one who would manage their money donations, make needed purchases, and distribute money to the Disciples as required.

How could Judas sacrifice three years of friendship with the Messiah to turn around and betray Him? Could it have been greed? That is a possibility; however, thirty pieces of silver wasn't very much money in those days.

Even though the Sadducees were highly motivated to get rid of Jesus, they didn't think He was worth using a more significant amount of their funds.

As Christians, we firmly believe the Blood of Jesus is priceless. But Judas and the Sadducees seemed to think thirty pieces of silver was all our Lord and Savior was worth.

Was Judas trying to force Jesus to become the kind of Messiah who fights off the Romans?

That is possible. The Sadducees, the Pharisees, and a large group of the Jews concluded that Jesus, that humble man of Nazareth, couldn't have been the Messiah as He didn't act or dress like a king. They expected Him to free them from the Romans who ruled over the Jews with an 'iron fist.' Instead, all Jesus wanted to do was teach everybody to Love God and Love all humankind.

Perhaps Judas had pictured himself as the right-hand helper of a rich man like King David. Being Treasurer for a king sounds a lot more prestigious than a money manager for a homeless man who does nothing but wander from place to place, healing people.

Or maybe Disciple John and the future writer of the Book of Mark were right that Judas allowed the devil to wiggle his way in, making him believe that it would be wise to betray Jesus. After all, Judas had already stolen money from his friends.

It would be inaccurate to say, "*The Devil made me do it.*" Satan cannot make anybody do anything. But he will do his utmost to persuade you. So, when Judas felt disappointed that Jesus didn't fit his idea of what a Messiah should be, Satan tempted Judas to do what was wrong and evil instead of right and good.

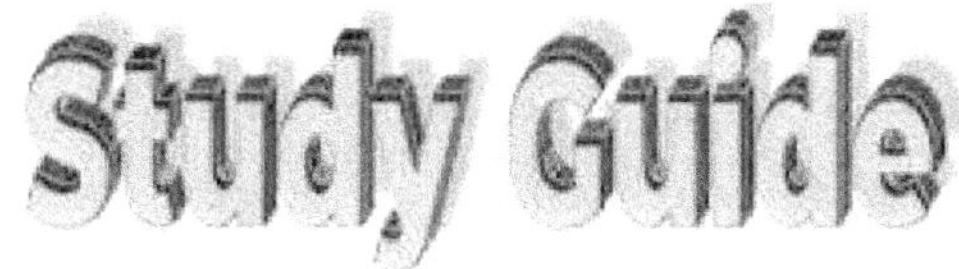

1. Explain your theory about why Judas chose to betray Jesus.

2. Explain in what ways King David's Psalm 109 aka Judas Psalm (described previously) and Psalm 41:9 (see bottom of this page) applied to Jesus.

> Role-play: Act it out or Journal about it. Group can Brainstorm additional ideas and suggestions of **W.W.J.D. (What Would Jesus Do)**.
> Two Actors: Jesus and King David.
> Plot: The two men share what they each experienced when a person they trusted betrayed them. Jesus should then teach King David how to forgive.

3. Disciple Peter asked Jesus how many times he must forgive someone who sinned against him. See what Jesus said as you read the Bible story called "The Parable of the Unmerciful Servant" in Matthew 18:21 to 35. Group Discussion or Journal about it. You might even want to act out the parable.

4. Think back to a time in your life when you felt betrayed by someone you trusted. Picture Jesus sitting down with you as you discuss what happened to you that day, why that person did that to you, and how you reacted. Contemplate how Jesus would advise you to proceed.

> Role-play: Act it out or Journal about it. Group can Brainstorm additional ideas and suggestions of **W.W.J.D. (What Would Jesus Do)**.
> Three Actors: Jesus, You and a Volunteer to play the role of that friend.
> Plot for 1st Skit: Reenact the negative interaction with your friend. Meet with Jesus.
> Plot for 2nd Skit: Both of you consider W.W.J.D. Then, act it out the positive way. A few options you might wish to try: Setting firm boundaries. Walking away if needed. Come up with a WIN-WIN Outcome. Apologize for reacting badly. Be gracious about accepting your friend's apology. Give them one more chance to be a better friend. Get verbal support from family or friends. Pray together. Meet with Jesus to counsel you, forgive you, and teach you to do better.

> ## All Bible References to Judas Iscariot
> - Matthew 10:1-4; Matthew 26:6-13; 14-16; 20-25; 46-50; Matthew 27:1-10
> - Mark 3:13-19; Mark 14:3-11; 18-21; 42-46
> - Luke 6:12-16; Luke 22:1-6; 20-23; 47-48
> - John 6:61-71; John 12:1-8; John 13:2; 10-11; 18-30; John 17:12
> - Acts 1:12-26 (*Details about a replacement disciple for Judas Iscariot*)
>
> **Psalm 41:9** Even my close friend, someone I trusted, one who shared my bread, has turned against me.

5. Read and discuss this Bible verse of what God told Moses to teach the Jews.

6. The authors of the Books of John and Mark said Judas Iscariot had invited the devil (or Satan) in to influence him to do what is evil. We know that Judas stole money from their group funds, he grumbled about some of the things that Jesus said or did, and he betrayed Jesus. Discuss or journal about how easy or hard you think it was for Satan to tempt Judas to do these things.

7. Discuss or journal about any time you might have invited Satan in to tempt you to gossip, bully, hit, slap, kick, tease in a mean way, lie, steal, do that 'ATTITUDE THING' with grown-ups, call names, refuse to do chores, etc.

8. Read King Solomon's Bible verse from Proverbs 16:27. That verse was pulled from the Living Bible, the New International, and King's James Version. Discuss or journal about how this verse applies to Judas.

9. Discuss or journal how this verse might have ever applied to you. Determine ways you can demand Satan to leave you alone in the Holy Name of Jesus.

10. Discuss or journal about how this verse applies to many things you view on the news, in war zones, on any Social Media sight, at school, work, home, with Persecuted Christians, etc. Find ways to pray for Jesus to influence that person to be eager to do what is pleasing to God instead of the Devil.

JESUS SADLY ASKED, "JUDAS, MUST YOU BETRAY ME WITH A KISS?"

He that betrayed Jesus had arrived.

Examine 4 Gospels for Clues (KJV)

Matthew 26:46-47	Mark 14:42-43	Luke	John 18:1-2
46 Rise, let us be going: behold, he is at hand that doth betray me.	42 Rise up, let us go; lo, he that betrayeth me is at hand.	No Reference to this Topic. 	1 When Jesus had spoken these words, he went forth with his disciples over the brook Cedron, where was a garden, into the which he entered, and his disciples.
47 And while he yet spake, lo, Judas, one of the twelve, came, and with him a great multitude with swords and staves, from the chief priests and elders of the people.	43 And immediately, while he yet spake, cometh Judas, one of the twelve, and with him a great multitude with swords and staves, from the chief priests and the scribes and the elders.		2 And Judas also, which betrayed him, knew the place: for Jesus ofttimes resorted thither with his disciples.

Judas said, "Bind tight whomever I kiss."

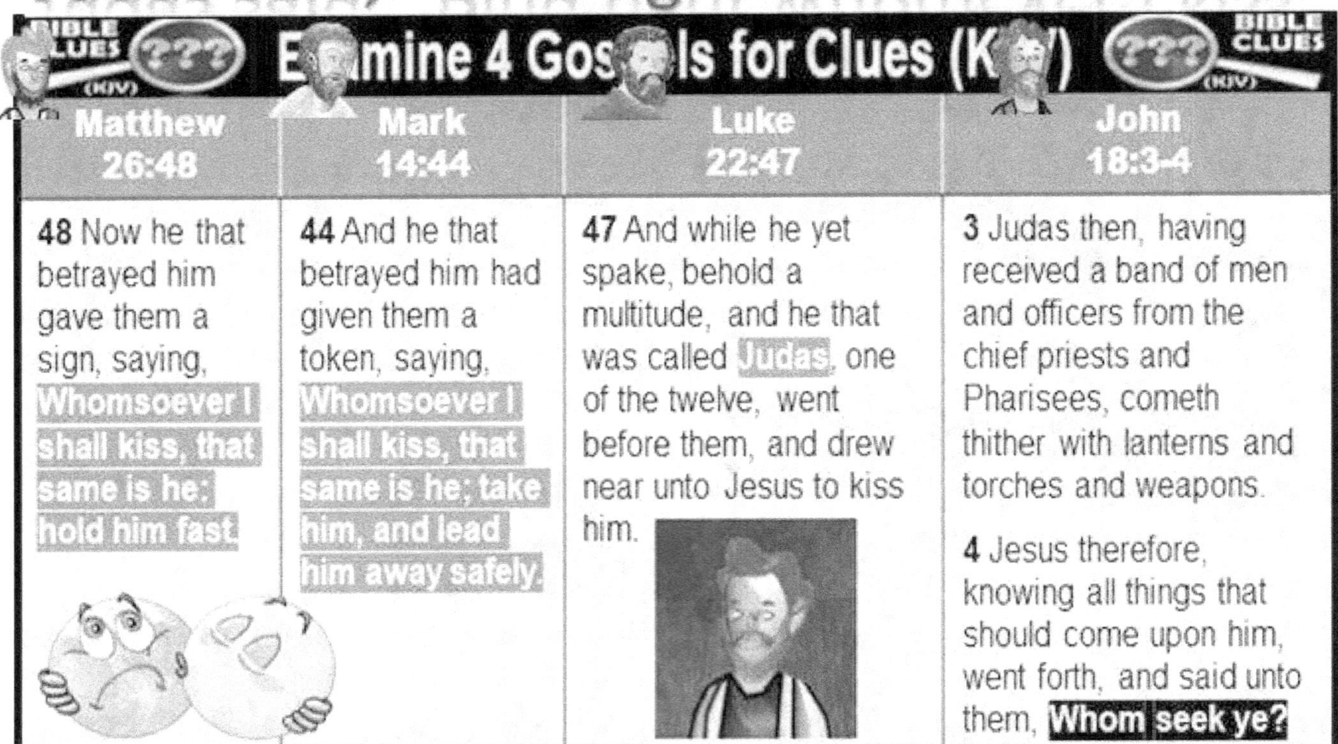

Matthew 26:48	Mark 14:44	Luke 22:47	John 18:3-4
48 Now he that betrayed him gave them a sign, saying, Whomsoever I shall kiss, that same is he: hold him fast.	44 And he that betrayed him had given them a token, saying, Whomsoever I shall kiss, that same is he; take him, and lead him away safely.	47 And while he yet spake, behold a multitude, and he that was called Judas, one of the twelve, went before them, and drew near unto Jesus to kiss him.	3 Judas then, having received a band of men and officers from the chief priests and Pharisees, cometh thither with lanterns and torches and weapons. 4 Jesus therefore, knowing all things that should come upon him, went forth, and said unto them, Whom seek ye?

With the understanding that a kiss of greeting was a common courtesy demonstrating honor and respect, the fact that Judas intended to use a kiss to betray Jesus to the soldiers was a double betrayal.

Betraying Son of Man with a Kiss

Examine 4 Gospels for Clues (KJV)

Matthew 26:49-50	Mark 14:45-46	Luke 22:48	John 18:4-5
49 And forthwith he came to Jesus, and said, **Hail, master**; and kissed him. 50 And Jesus said unto him, **Friend, wherefore art thou come?** Then came they, and laid hands on Jesus and took him.	45 And as soon as he was come, he goeth straightway to him, and saith, **Master, master**, and kissed him. 46 And they laid their hands on him, and took him.	48 But Jesus said unto him, **Judas, betrayest thou the Son of man with a kiss?**	4 Jesus therefore, ... said unto them, **Whom seek ye?** 5 They answered him, **Jesus of Nazareth**. Jesus saith unto them, **I am he.** And Judas also, which betrayed him, stood with them.

At Jesus' voice, they all fell down!

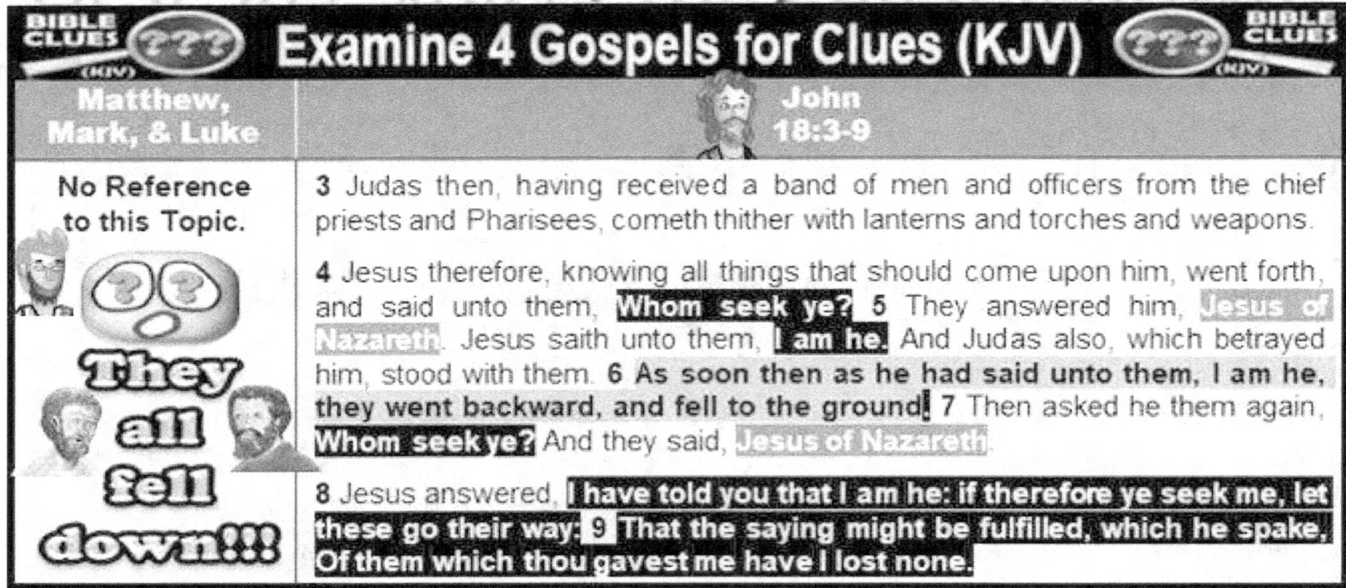

3 Judas then, having received a band of men and officers from the chief priests and Pharisees, cometh thither with lanterns and torches and weapons.

4 Jesus therefore, knowing all things that should come upon him, went forth, and said unto them, Whom seek ye? **5** They answered him, Jesus of Nazareth. Jesus saith unto them, I am he. And Judas also, which betrayed him, stood with them. **6 As soon then as he had said unto them, I am he, they went backward, and fell to the ground.** **7** Then asked he them again, Whom seek ye? And they said, Jesus of Nazareth.

8 Jesus answered, I have told you that I am he: if therefore ye seek me, let these go their way: **9** That the saying might be fulfilled, which he spake, Of them which thou gavest me have I lost none.

Judas was likely trying to recreate Jesus in his own image. He longed for Jesus to call down His Legion of Angels to overpower the Romans. He thought, "If I was the Messiah, that is what I would do." As he hurried to hide himself behind the Sanhedrin soldiers, to his disgust, he saw that Jesus was peacefully intending to allow them to arrest Him.

Suddenly, a strange thing happened. Right after Jesus said, "I am he," every Pharisee and soldier toppled over. The Bible doesn't inform us if they toppled over backward like petrified logs or if they merely crumpled to the ground backward. The wave of majestic and compassionate Love spiraling out of Jesus caused every man to fall so that Judas' hiding place was exposed. Judas probably looked at the fallen men, the sky, and then Jesus to silently urge Him to call down His Angels. Jesus sighed as He shook His head 'NO.'

When Judas saw the shock, hurt, and righteous anger on the faces of the eleven other Disciples he had traveled with for three years; he realized he had burned the bridge connecting them to him. Judas also felt he had severed any claim to Jesus' continued affection. He had no way of comprehending Jesus had already forgiven him and all other people their sins.

As Judas exited the Garden of Gethsemane and the three years of his life where he served as one of Jesus' twelve Disciples, he likely spent some time reflecting on what he witnessed. For example, around the period when King Herod beheaded John the Baptist, Jesus sent out His Disciples, two-by-two, to heal the sick and drive out demons. Judas got to experience the power of being able to heal, in the name of Jesus, with both his hands and his words. He even got to drive out demons. The Bible describes this mission trip in **Matthew 9:35-38, 10:1-42, & 11:1**, **Mark 6:6-12**, and **Luke 9:1-9**. So, Judas got to experience all of that. And yet, he could not let go of his personal agenda that Jesus' primary purpose should have been overthrowing the power of Rome.

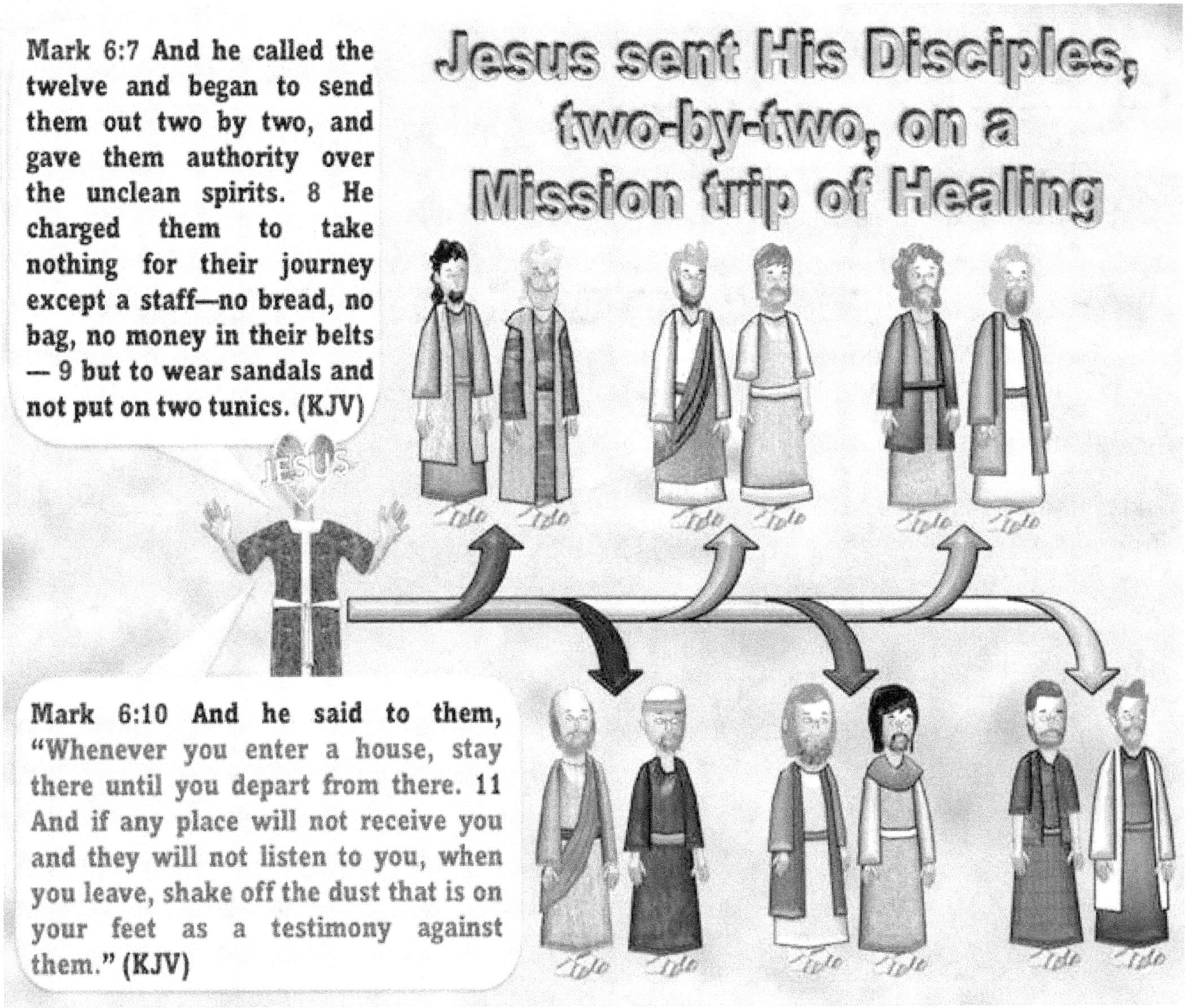

Mark 6:7 And he called the twelve and began to send them out two by two, and gave them authority over the unclean spirits. 8 He charged them to take nothing for their journey except a staff—no bread, no bag, no money in their belts — 9 but to wear sandals and not put on two tunics. (KJV)

Mark 6:10 And he said to them, "Whenever you enter a house, stay there until you depart from there. 11 And if any place will not receive you and they will not listen to you, when you leave, shake off the dust that is on your feet as a testimony against them." (KJV)

The other anomaly was that Judas could not grasp that he had been entertaining the presence of a demon for the last few days or weeks. John documented this fact in **John 6:70** and **John 13:27**. Luke documented this in **Luke 22:3**. Judas likely had been listening to Satan whispering in his ear to disrespect and betray Jesus. What would Satan suggest that he do next?

Judas realized that the connection and trust with the eleven Disciples was gone. The Disciples would no longer trust him as their "keeper of the money bag."(John 12:6)

In addition, Disciple John, son of Zebedee, became aware of these facts about Judas. John stated in **John 12:6**:

"He did not say this because he cared about the poor but because he was a thief; as keeper of the money bag, he used to help himself to what was put into it."

So, besides the funds remaining in that money bag, Judas would receive no further financial help from that source.

Across the field of fallen bodies, Jesus viewed Judas, the Pharisees, and the Sanhedrin soldiers as chicks He would gladly gather under His protective wings. He viewed them with compassionate Love. Through Judas' filter of fear and guilt, he misinterpreted Jesus' gaze as one of convicting condemnation.

Perhaps Judas Iscariot hoped that the Pharisees would be so grateful for his services that they would give him gainful employment. Instead, I believe that after Judas kissed Jesus, identifying him as their desired victim, Judas did not get his desired reception. I imagine one of the Pharisees hissed, "Are you sure that is Him and not one of His Disciples willing to martyr themselves to save Him?" After Judas guaranteed that it was indeed Jesus they would be arresting, they probably had no further use for him. They intended to ignore Judas from that day forward.

Judas was not a lost cause. He could have sincerely repented of betraying Christ and embezzling funds. Jesus nailed those sins on the Cross along with His body. Once the Disciples received the gift of the Holy Spirit on the Day of Pentecost, 50 days after Jesus' resurrection, as described in **Acts 2:1-31**, the Disciples would be enabled to forgive Judas.

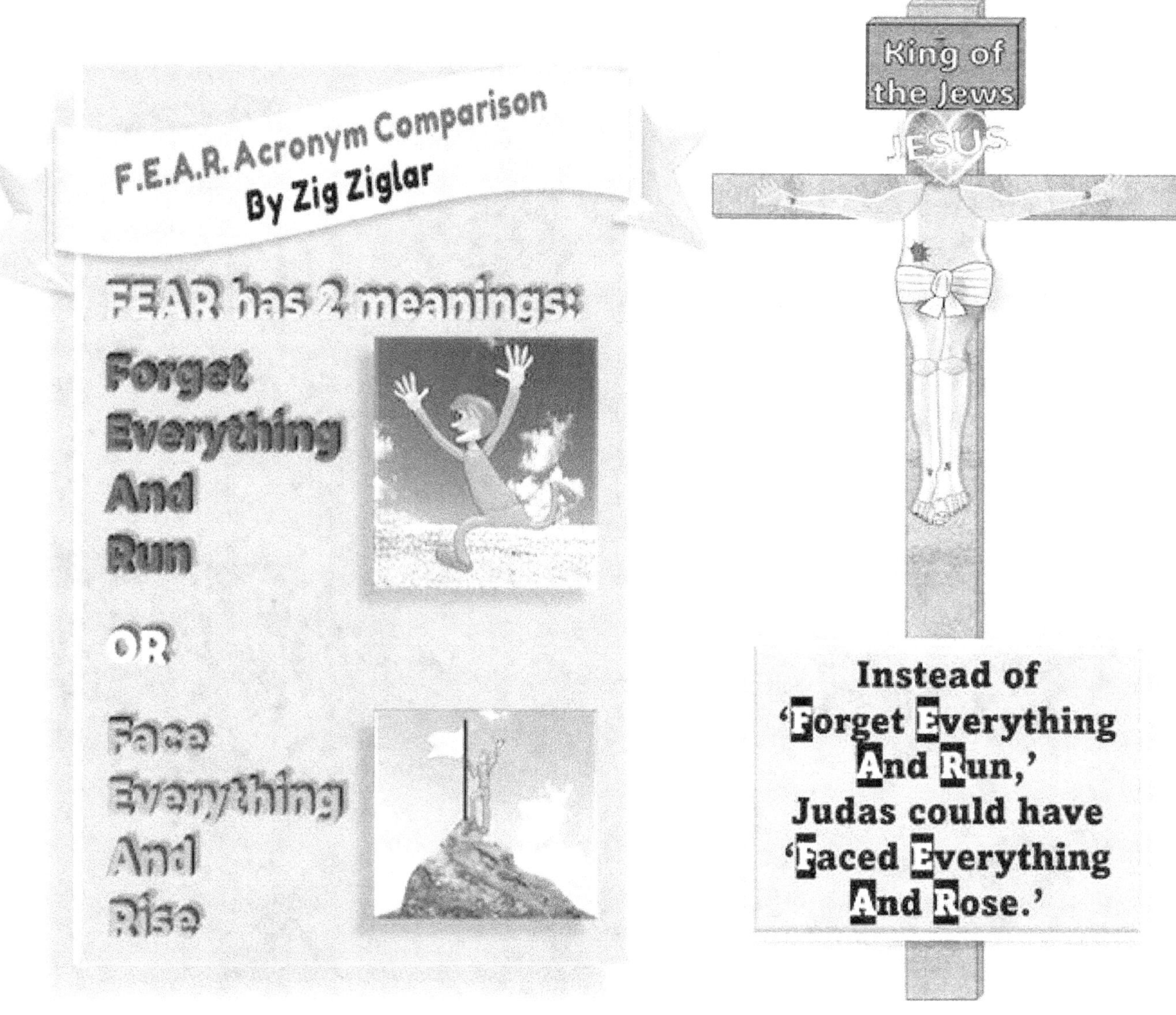

For example, recall that the born-again Apostle Paul, back when he was still Saul of Tarsus, murdered and tortured Christians. When Paul sincerely repented and dedicated himself to 'paying it forward' to demonstrate his sincere remorse, the Disciples and Christ-followers learned to forgive and trust Paul over time due to the gift of the Holy Spirit. See **Acts 9:1-22**.

So, Judas did not have to die. He did not have to kill himself. There was another option. There was a better choice. He could have 'paid it forward' on behalf of Christ.

There is always a better alternative than the taking of your own life. That was so unnecessary. That was such a waste! After all, Jesus truly Loved Judas Iscariot just as He sincerely and compassionately Loves every person on this planet: Past, current, and future.

 Satan might even have egged on Judas to commit the sin of self-murder, for we know with certainty that Satan did not want Judas to try to continue following Jesus.

In the same way, Jesus is willing to forgive each of you who may have become a **NEGATIVE INFLUENCER** or who may even have made a pact with the devil to receive fame or fortune or both. Jesus will gladly take you back into the fold if you will only be willing to do these four (4) things:

1. **Stop sinning in this manner.**
2. **Sincerely repent.**
3. **Ask Jesus to forgive you.**
4. **Accept Jesus as your Lord and Savior instead of Satan.**

It is not too late for you to have your soul redeemed. But do not wait too long, as we are not guaranteed tomorrow. If you wait too long and die prematurely, you'll end up spending eternity in solo cells in hell instead of in joyful fellowship in Heaven.

PUT AWAY YOUR SWORD!

Swords won't prevent Jesus' suffering.

Examine 4 Gospels for Clues (KJV)

Matthew 26:51-52	Mark 14:47	Luke 22:49-51	John 18:10-11
51 And, behold, one of them which were with Jesus stretched out his hand, and drew his sword, and struck a servant of the high priest's, and smote off his ear. 52 Then said Jesus unto him, **Put up again thy sword into his place: for all they that take the sword shall perish with the sword.**	47 And one of them that stood by drew a sword, and smote a servant of the high priest, and cut off his ear.  Bloody Sword	49 When they which were about him saw what would follow, they said unto him, **Lord, shall we smite with the sword?** 50 And one of them smote the servant of the high priest, and cut off his right ear. 51 And Jesus answered and said, **Suffer ye thus far.** And he touched his ear, and healed him.	10 Then Simon Peter having a sword drew it, and smote the high priest's servant, and cut off his right ear. The servant's name was Malchus. 11 Then said Jesus unto Peter, **Put up thy sword into the sheath: the cup which my Father hath given me, shall I not drink it?**

Examine 4 Gospels for Clues (KJV)

BIBLE CLUES (KJV) ??? | ??? BIBLE CLUES (KJV)

| Matthew 26:53-54 | Mark & Luke | John 18:6-9 |

Matthew 26:53-54

53 Thinkest thou that I cannot now pray to my Father, and he shall presently give me more than twelve legions of angels?

There are 6,000 Angels per legion.

6000
X 12
72,000 Angels

54 But how then shall the scriptures be fulfilled, that thus it must be?

Mark & Luke

No Reference to this Topic.

REMEZ — Hidden Messages

WIKIPEDIA QUOTE: "Esdras is in the Apocrypha of the King James Version, and Pope Clement VIII placed it in an appendix to the Vulgate along with 3 Esdras and the Prayer of Manasseh 'lest they perish entirely'."

2 Esdras 2:23 Wheresoever thou findest the dead, take them and bury them, and I will give thee the first place in my resurrection. 24 Abide still, O my people, and take thy rest, for thy quietness still come. 25 Nourish thy children, O thou good nurse; stablish their feet. 26 As for the servants whom I have given thee, there shall not one of them perish; for I will require them from among thy number. 27 Be not weary: for when the day of trouble and heaviness cometh, others shall weep and be sorrowful, but thou shalt be merry and have abundance. 28 The heathen shall envy thee, but they shall be able to do nothing against thee, saith the Lord. 29 My hands shall cover thee, so that thy children shall not see hell. (KJV)

John 18:6-9

6 As soon then as he had said unto them, I am he they went backward, and fell to the ground.

7 Then asked he them again, Whom seek ye? And they said, Jesus of Nazareth.

8 Jesus answered, I have told you that I am he: if therefore ye seek me, let these go their way: 9 That the saying might be fulfilled, which he spake, Of them which thou gavest me have I lost none.

Peter must have felt so confused that night. The Sanhedrin were in the process of arresting Jesus, the man he had faithfully followed for the last three years. Yet, when Peter tried to play the hero by slicing off the ear of one of the men seeking to harm his master, he did not receive thanks. Instead, Jesus reprimanded him. Were they all meant to stand back and allow Jesus to be tortured and killed?

He felt shame that he, John, and James hadn't managed to stay awake when Jesus was wailing and praying earlier. At the Last Supper, Jesus had also predicted that Peter would deny Him three times before the cock crowed. He felt all twisted up inside. What was he supposed to think or do now?

We learn from the Bible verses below that he intended to follow at a distance. So, he must have hidden behind an Olive Tree and watched what unfolded.

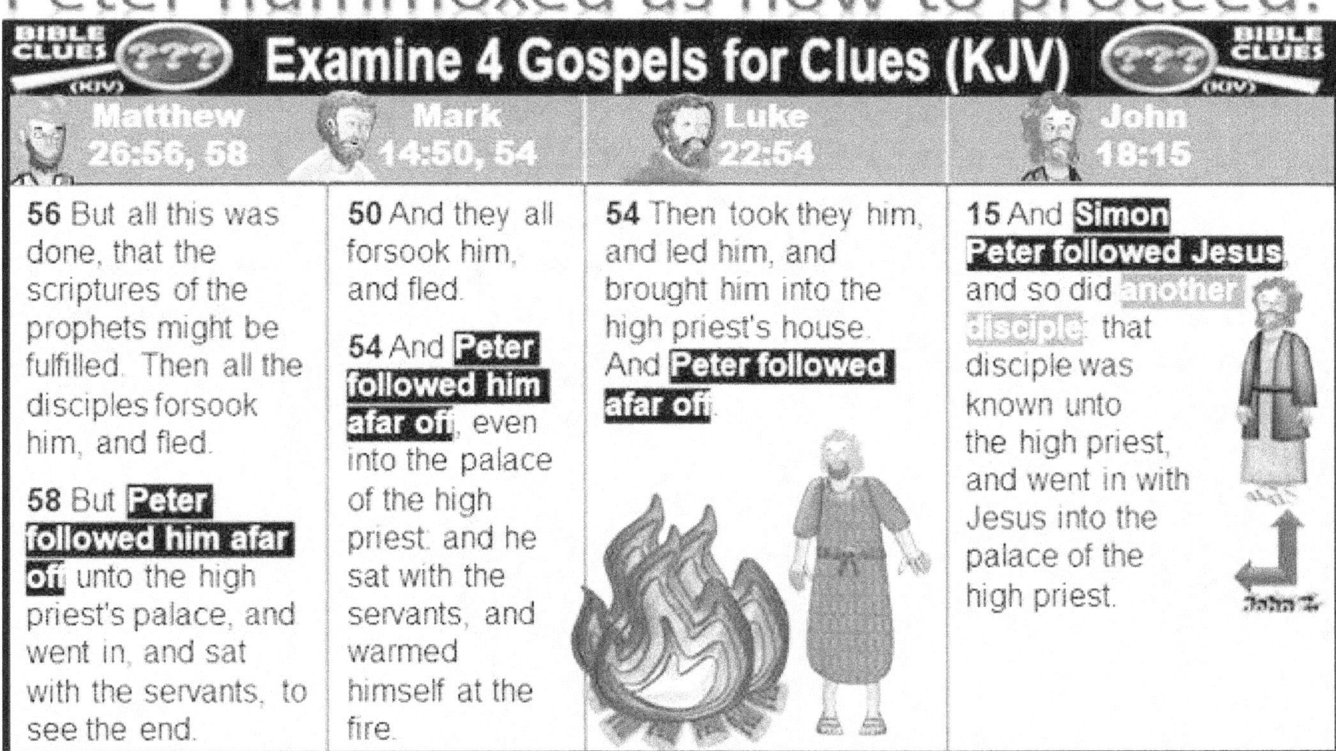

ARE YOU TRYING TO CAPTURE ME AS IF I WAS A THIEF?

Treating Jesus like He was a thief

Examine 4 Gospels for Clues (KJV)

Matthew 26:55-56	Mark 14:48-49	Luke 22:52-53	John
55 In that same hour said Jesus to the multitudes, Are ye come out as against a thief with swords and staves for to take me? I sat daily with you teaching in the temple, and ye laid no hold on me. **56** But all this was done, that the scriptures of the prophets might be fulfilled. ...	**48** And Jesus answered and said unto them, Are ye come out, as against a thief, with swords and with staves to take me? **49** I was daily with you in the temple teaching, and ye took me not: but the scriptures must be fulfilled.	**52** Then Jesus said unto the chief priests, and captains of the temple, and the elders, which were come to him, Be ye come out, as against a thief, with swords and staves? **53** When I was daily with you in the temple, ye stretched forth no hands against me: but this is your hour, and the power of darkness.	No Reference to this Topic **REMEZ Hidden Message** Psalm 31:13 For I hear many whispering, "Terror on every side!" They conspire against me and plot to take my life. Lamentations 4:18 People stalked us at every step, so we could not walk in our streets. Our end was near, our days were numbered, for our end had come. Lamentations 4:19 Our pursuers were swifter than eagles in the sky; they chased us over the mountains and lay in wait for us in the desert. **20** The Lord's anointed, our very life breath, was caught in their traps. We thought that under his shadow we would live among the nations. **(NIV)**

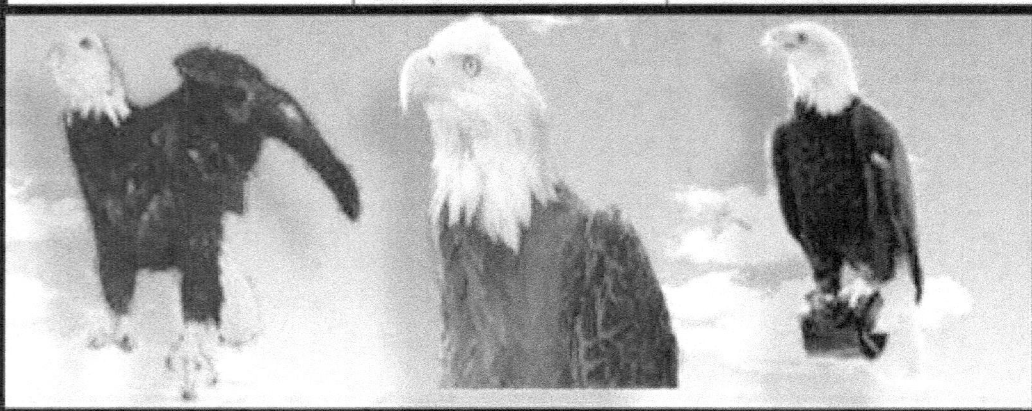

THE DISCIPLES FLED IN TERROR

Disciples ran away in fear.

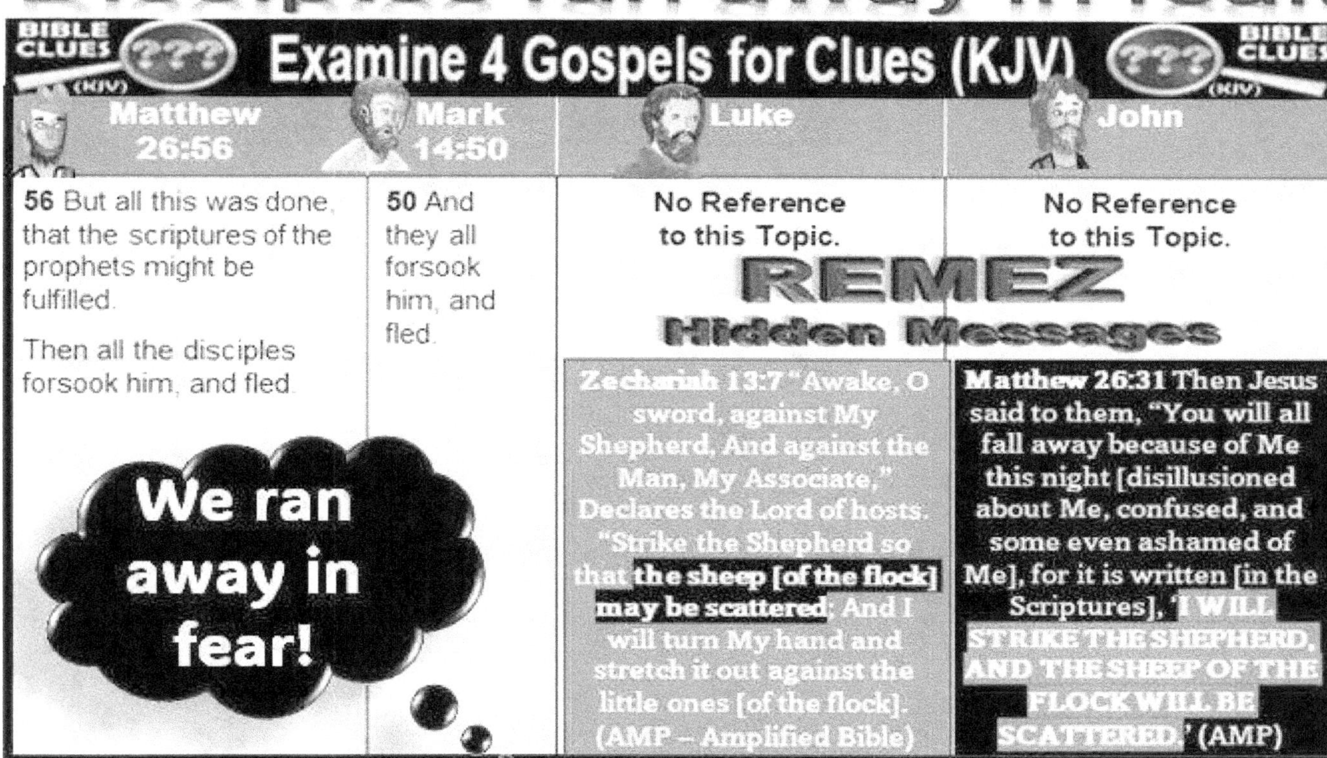

Matthew 26:56	Mark 14:50	Luke	John
56 But all this was done, that the scriptures of the prophets might be fulfilled. Then all the disciples forsook him, and fled.	50 And they all forsook him, and fled.	No Reference to this Topic.	No Reference to this Topic.

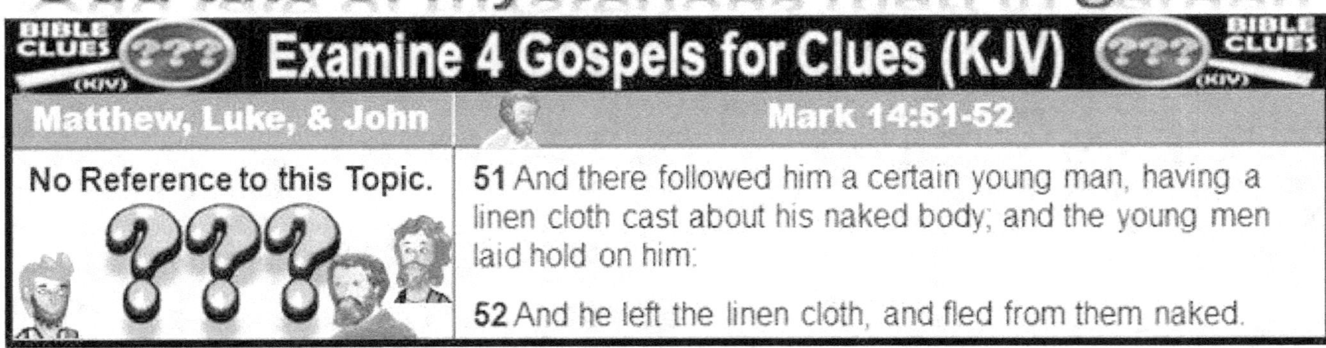

Odd tale of mysterious man in garden

BIBLE CLUES (KJV) ??? Examine 4 Gospels for Clues (KJV) ??? BIBLE CLUES (KJV)	
Matthew, Luke, & John	**Mark 14:51-52**
No Reference to this Topic. 	51 And there followed him a certain young man, having a linen cloth cast about his naked body; and the young men laid hold on him: 52 And he left the linen cloth, and fled from them naked.

No one knows anything more about this young man. He, whoever he is, is never mentioned again in the Bible.

Did he come to the Garden of Gethsemane in need of healing? Perhaps he had a demon and hoped that Jesus could free him from it. Was he robbed and that is why he had nothing on beyond that linen cloth? Where did he go after he ran away? This is a complete mystery.

As stated above, only Jesus knew about his story.

PETER FOLLOWED AT A DISTANCE

After the Disciples ran away, we only know about the activities of Peter and Disciple John. The rest might have returned to the Upper Room.

Disciples Peter & John followed Jesus.

Examine 4 Gospels for Clues (KJV)

Matthew 26:57-58	Mark 14:53-54	Luke	John 18:15
57 And they that had laid hold on Jesus led him away to Caiaphas the high priest, where the scribes and the elders were assembled. **58** But **Peter** followed him afar off unto the high priest's palace, and went in, and sat with the servants, to see the end.	53 And they led Jesus away to the high priest: and with him were assembled all the chief priests and the elders and the scribes. 54 And **Peter** followed him afar off, even into the palace of the high priest: and he sat with the servants, and warmed himself at the fire.	**No Reference to this Topic.**	15 And **Simon Peter followed Jesus**, and so did **another disciple**: that disciple was known unto the high priest, and went in with Jesus into the palace of the high priest.

1. Read King Solomon's Bible verse below. Describe all the ways this applies to what happened between Jesus and Judas.

Proverbs 27:6 Faithful are the wounds of a friend, but the kisses of an enemy are deceitful. (KJV)

2. Why do you think the Sanhedrin insisted that Judas choose a way to correctly identify Jesus?

3. When Peter pulled out a sword, describe his motives and intentions for that moment.

4. Why do you think Jesus urged Peter to put away his sword?

5. If Jesus had not healed the ear of the High Priest's servant, what do you think would have happened to Peter?

6. Why do you think the Sanhedrin sent hundreds of soldiers to arrest Jesus?

7. What do you think would have happened to the Disciples if they had remained when the soldiers arrested Jesus?

8. What is your theory about the naked young man described in the book of Mark 14:51-52?

9. Why do you think Peter chose to follow Jesus at a distance? What do you suppose he was hoping to see or accomplish?

10. Where do you think Judas chose to be after the soldiers arrested Jesus?

11. What do you think was going through Jesus' head after He was arrested? What emotions do you think He was feeling when this happened?

12. What do you think the other Disciples were thinking or feeling when they saw what happened to Jesus?

1ST OF 6 TRIALS FOR JESUS

They held the first trial for Jesus at the home of the former High Priest, Annas. Even though the procurator deposed Annas from that position in 15 AD, he still had a lot of political power and influence. According to Wikipedia, all five of his sons and his current son-in-law served as high priests for varying lengths of time. His son-in-law Caiaphas would hold that office for the longest stretch. He began his term in 18 AD and served as High Priest until 36 AD.

1st Trial for Jesus – Annas' Residence

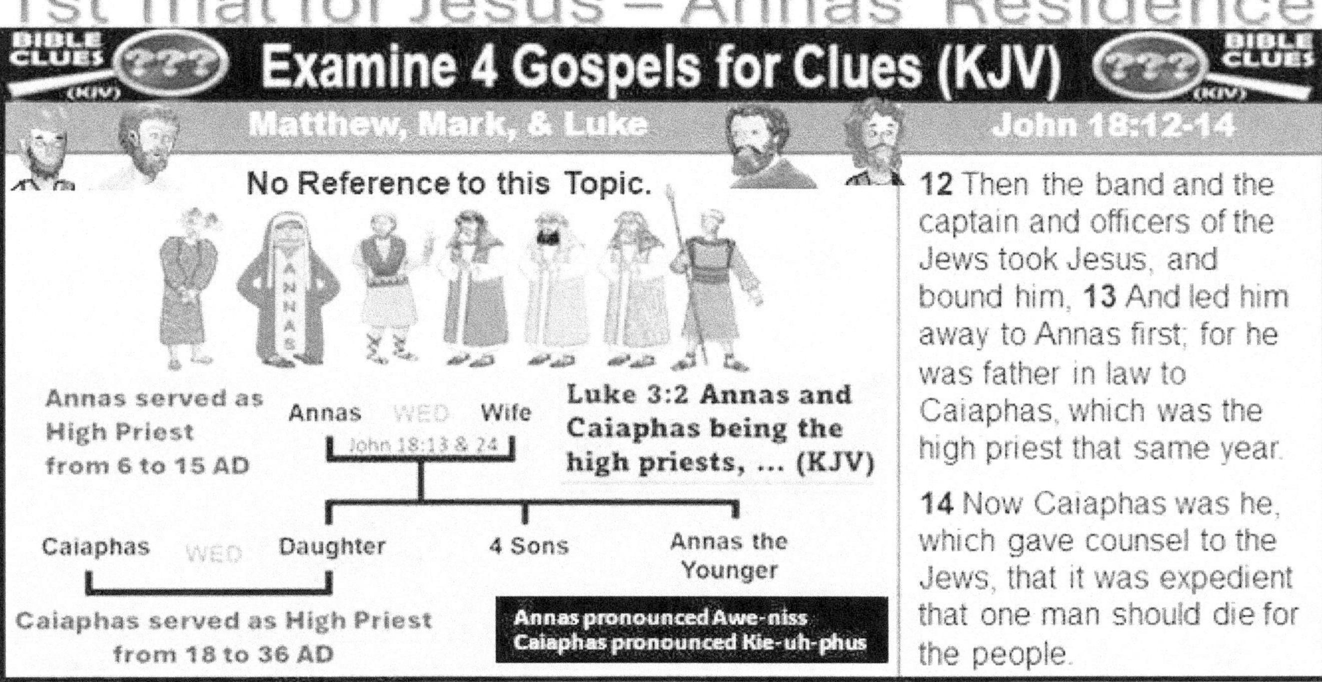

John 18:19 **The high priest then asked Jesus of his disciples, and of his doctrine.** (KJV)

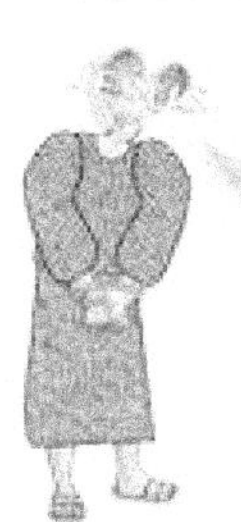

Describe your Disciples and your Doctrine.

John 18:20 **Jesus answered him, I spake openly to the world; I ever taught in the synagogue, and in the temple, whither the Jews always resort; and in secret have I said nothing. 21 Why askest thou me? ask them which heard me, what I have said unto them: behold, they know what I said.** (KJV)

John 18:22 And when he had thus spoken, one of the officers which stood by struck Jesus with the palm of his hand, saying, Answerest thou the high priest so? (KJV)

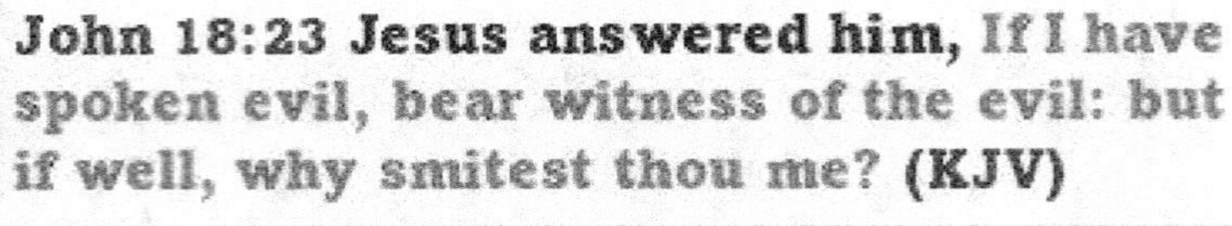

John 18:24 Now Annas had sent him bound unto Caiaphas the high priest. (KJV)

That was the end of the first trial.

Let's reflect for a moment on two of the previous verses:

John 18:22 And when he had thus spoken, one of the officers which stood by struck Jesus with the palm of his hand, saying, Answerest thou the high priest so? (KJV)

John 18:23 Jesus answered him, If I have spoken evil, bear witness of the evil: but if well, why smitest thou me? (KJV)

Every WORD in the Holy Bible is intentional and carefully planned by the Triune God. As followers of Christ, we are responsible for reading between the lines. To ensure we interpret all of this correctly, we have the Holy Spirit as our teacher and guide to illuminate our understanding and comprehension.

Now, picture yourself standing in the place of Jesus. Being slapped, with or without reason, is **TRIGGERING**. I firmly believe that even if Jesus' hands were not tied together, if he raised his arm(s) at all, it was with the intention of taking this troubled man into his compassionately Loving embrace. Just like Jesus would have gathered His Disciples under His protective wings, He would have done the same for every person in Annas' home.

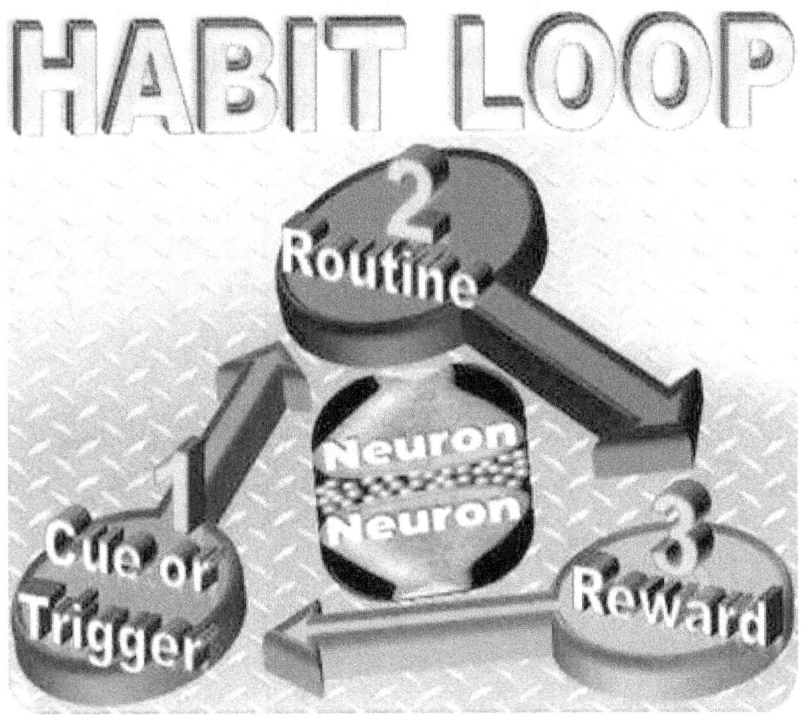

Jesus' matter-of-fact response to Annas **TRIGGERED** the Sanhedrin officer. His **ROUTINE** was to slap or punch the person he perceived as the offender to the leader he served, Annas. However, he did not get his anticipated **REWARD**. Both he and Annas wanted to see Jesus lose his composure, cry out, or try to fight back in some way. They did not receive any of that. Instead, Jesus did not allow himself to be **TRIGGERED** or to take offense. He answered them calmly, with respectful composure. Disappointed, Annas sent Jesus to be tried by his son-in-law, Caiaphas.

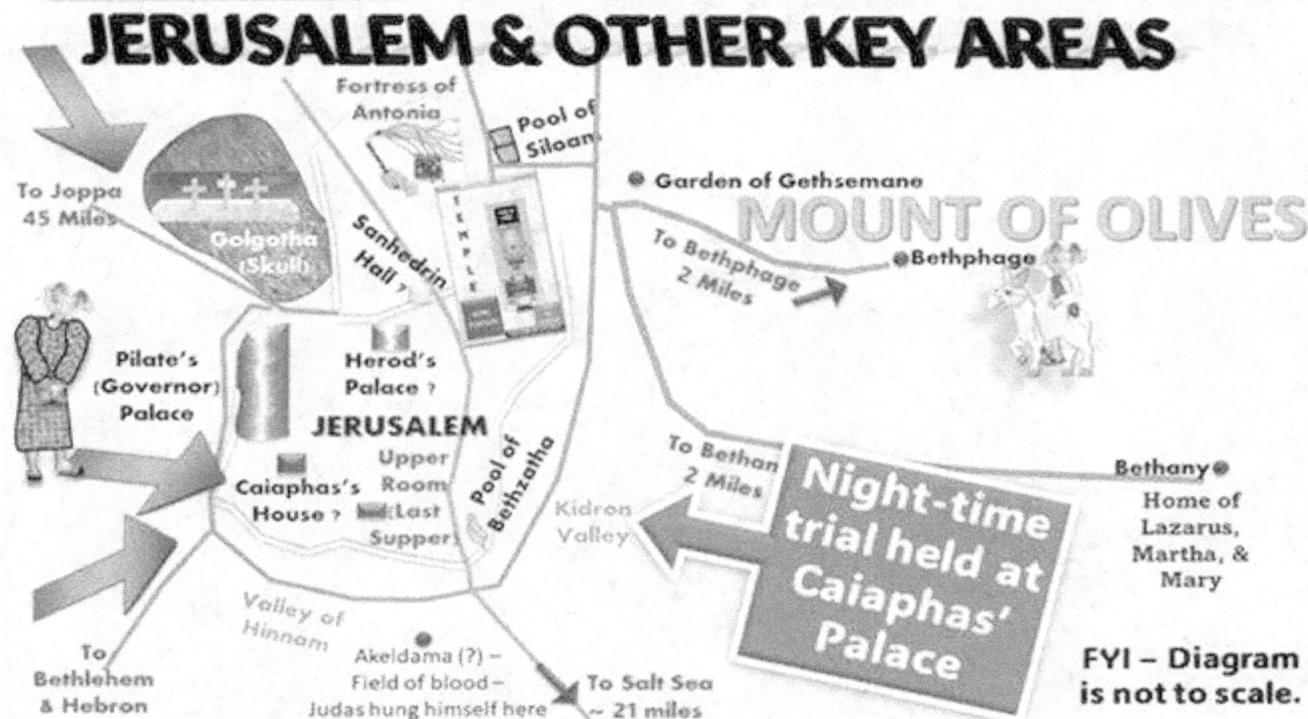

2nd Trial for Jesus – Caiaphas' Palace

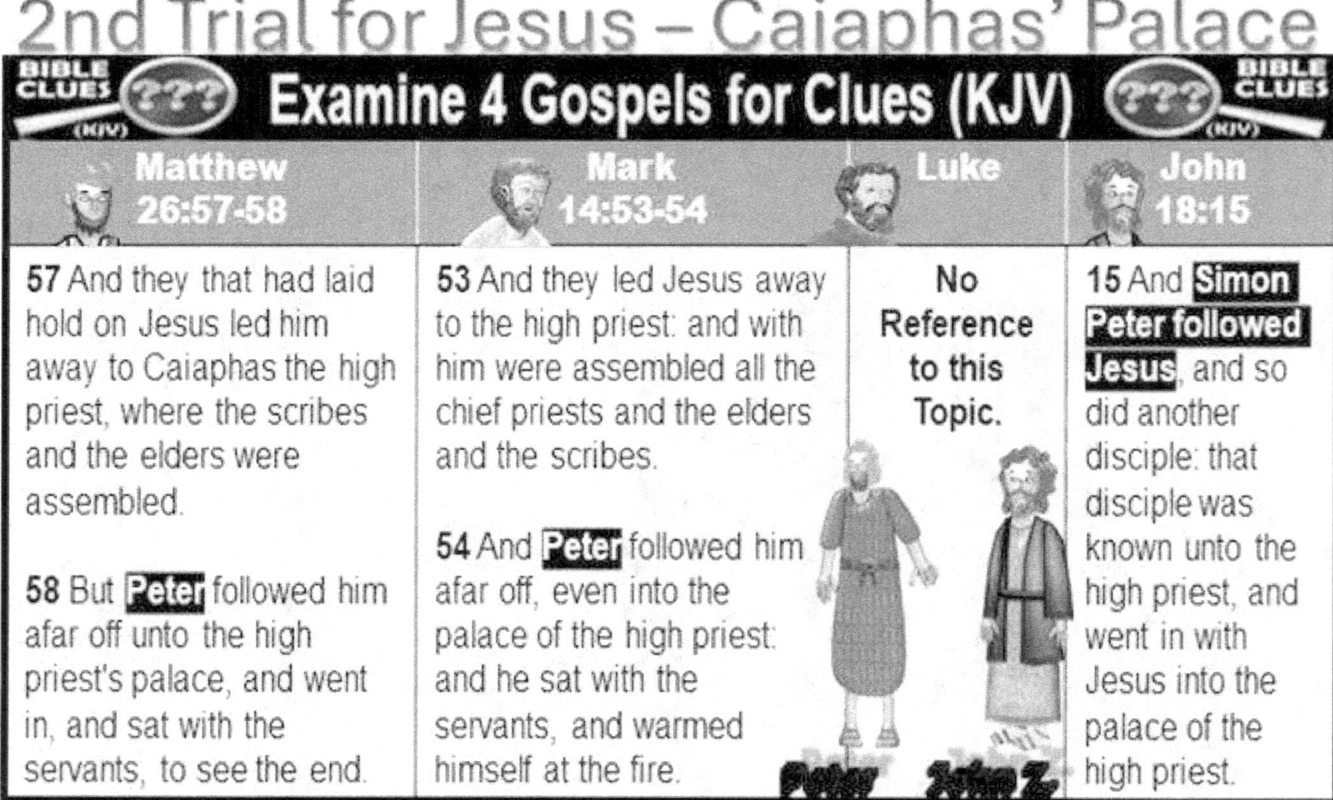

Examine 4 Gospels for Clues (KJV)

Matthew 26:57-58	Mark 14:53-54	Luke	John 18:15
57 And they that had laid hold on Jesus led him away to Caiaphas the high priest, where the scribes and the elders were assembled. 58 But Peter followed him afar off unto the high priest's palace, and went in, and sat with the servants, to see the end.	53 And they led Jesus away to the high priest: and with him were assembled all the chief priests and the elders and the scribes. 54 And Peter followed him afar off, even into the palace of the high priest: and he sat with the servants, and warmed himself at the fire.	No Reference to this Topic.	15 And Simon Peter followed Jesus, and so did another disciple: that disciple was known unto the high priest, and went in with Jesus into the palace of the high priest.

It is possible that both Peter and John followed Jesus to the home of Annas but could not get entry. Next, they followed the crowd to the palace of Caiaphas, the current High Priest.

In **John 18:15**, we learn that Disciple John is known there. Perhaps, this was when John was still a full-time fisherman, along with his older brother James, both working for his father, Zebedee. John might have made deliveries to Caiaphas' kitchen so the palace residents would stay fully stocked with fish.

> **John 18:16 But Peter stood at the door without. Then went out that other disciple, which was known unto the high priest, and spake unto her that kept the door, and brought in Peter. (KJV)**

From **John 18:16**, we learn that there was a damsel in charge of the door. She appeared to recognize Peter as she said:

John 18:18 And the servants and officers stood there, who had made a fire of coals; for it was cold: and they warmed themselves: and Peter stood with them, and warmed himself. (KJV)

In the book of John, the above depiction was how John described the first of three denials by Peter about not knowing Christ Jesus. See how the other three Gospel books of Matthew, Mark, and Luke describe this same incident.

BIBLE CLUES — Examine 4 Gospels for Clues (KJV)

Matthew 26:69-70	Mark 14:66-68	Luke 22:55-57	John 18:17-18
69 Now Peter sat without in the palace: and a damsel came unto him, saying, Thou also wast with Jesus of Galilee. **70** But he denied before them all, saying, I know not what thou sayest.	**66** And as Peter was beneath in the palace, there cometh one of the maids of the high priest: **67** And when she saw Peter warming himself, she looked upon him, and said, And thou also wast with Jesus of Nazareth. **68** But he denied, saying, I know not, neither understand I what thou sayest. And he went out into the porch; and the cock crew.	**55** And when they had kindled a fire in the midst of the hall, and were set down together, Peter sat down among them. **56** But a certain maid beheld him as he sat by the fire, and earnestly looked upon him, and said, This man was also with him. **57** And he denied him, saying, Woman, I know him not.	**17** Then saith the damsel that kept the door unto Peter, Art not thou also one of this man's disciples? He saith, I am not. **18** And the servants and officers stood there, who had made a fire of coals; for it was cold: and they warmed themselves: and Peter stood with them, and warmed himself.

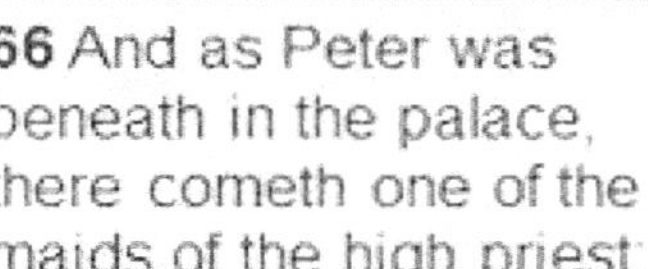

Compare the four Gospels for the description of Peter's 2nd denial of Christ.

 Peter's 2nd Denial of Knowing Jesus 

Examine 4 Gospels for Clues (KJV)

Matthew 26:71-72	Mark 14:69-70	Luke 22:58	John 18:25
71 And when he was gone out into the porch, another maid saw him, and said unto them that were there, This fellow was also with Jesus of Nazareth. **72** And again he denied with an oath, I do not know the man.	**69** And a maid saw him again, and began to say to them that stood by, This is one of them. **70** And he denied it again. … *(Verse 70 continues with 3rd denial.)*	**58** And after a little while another saw him, and said, Thou art also of them. And Peter said, 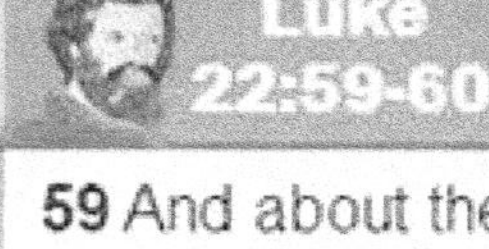	**25** And Simon Peter stood and warmed himself. They said therefore unto him, Art not thou also one of his disciples? He denied it, and said, I am not.

With Peter's third and final denial of Christ, we learn, in **Matthew 26:74** and **Mark 14:71**, that he even chose to curse and swear as he made that denial.

 Peter's 3rd Denial of Knowing Jesus

Examine 4 Gospels for Clues (KJV)

Matthew 26:73-74	Mark 14:70-71	Luke 22:59-60	John 18:26-27
73 And after a while came unto him they that stood by, and said to Peter, Surely thou also art one of them; for thy speech betrayeth thee. **74** Then began he to curse and to swear, saying, I know not the man. And immediately the cock crew.	**70** … And a little after, they that stood by said again to Peter, Surely thou art one of them: for thou art a Galilaean, and thy speech agreeth thereto. **71** But he began to curse and to swear, saying, I know not this man of whom ye speak.	**59** And about the space of one hour after another confidently affirmed, saying, Of a truth this fellow also was with him: for he is a Galilaean. **60** And Peter said, Man, I know not what thou sayest. And immediately, while he yet spake, the cock crew.	**26** One of the servants of the high priest, being his kinsman whose ear Peter cut off, saith, Did not I see thee in the garden with him? **27** Peter then denied again: and immediately the cock crew.

So, what happened next? What was the aftermath of those three denials? If I had been in Peter's shoes, what Luke described in **Luke 22:61** would have haunted my dreams for a very long time. See the re-play below.

Peter's 3rd Denial of Knowing Jesus
continued

Examine 4 Gospels for Clues (KJV)

Matthew 26:75	Mark 14:72	Luke 22:61-62	John 18:26-27
75 And Peter remembered the word of Jesus, which said unto him, Before the cock crow, thou shalt deny me thrice. And he went out, and wept bitterly.	72 And the second time the cock crew. And Peter called to mind the word that Jesus said unto him, Before the cock crow twice, thou shalt deny me thrice. And when he thought thereon, he wept.	61 And the Lord turned, and looked upon Peter. And Peter remembered the word of the Lord, how he had said unto him, Before the cock crow, thou shalt deny me thrice. 62 And Peter went out, and wept bitterly.	26 One of the servants of the high priest, being his kinsman whose ear Peter cut off, saith, Did not I see thee in the garden with him? 27 Peter then denied again: and immediately the cock crew.

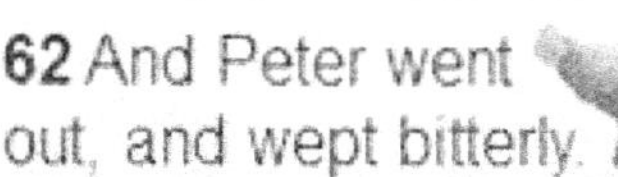

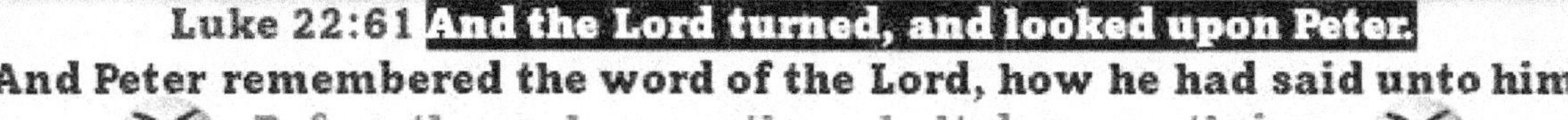

Luke 22:61 And the Lord turned, and looked upon Peter. And Peter remembered the word of the Lord, how he had said unto him, Before the cock crow, thou shalt deny me thrice. 62 And Peter went out, and wept bitterly. (KJV)

Here is what happened during the second trial for Jesus inside Caiaphas' palace. This trial was all about them seeking false witnesses to entrap Jesus.

Exodus 20:16 **9** **Thou shall not bear false witness.**

Examine 4 Gospels for Clues (KJV)

Matthew 26:59-61	Mark 14:55-59	Luke	John 18:24 & 28
59 Now the chief priests, and elders, and all the council, sought false witness against Jesus, to put him to death; 60 But found none: yea, though many false witnesses came, yet found they none. At the last came two false witnesses, 61 And said, This fellow said, I am able to destroy the temple of God, and to build it in three days.	55 And the chief priests and all the council sought for witness against Jesus to put him to death; and found none. 56 For many bare false witness against him, but their witness agreed not together. 57 And there arose certain, and bare false witness against him, saying, 58 We heard him say, I will destroy this temple that is made with hands, and within three days I will build another made without hands. 59 But neither so did their witness agree together.	No Reference to the trial that took place inside Caiaphas' palace. Instead, Luke describes the manner they began to torture Jesus after that trial.	24 Now Annas had sent him bound unto Caiaphas the high priest.

28 Then led they Jesus from Caiaphas unto the hall of judgment: and it was early; and they themselves went not into the judgment hall, lest they should be defiled; but that they might eat the **passover**.

Examine 4 Gospels for Clues (KJV)

Matthew 26:62-64	Mark 14:60-62	Luke	John
62 And the high priest arose, and said unto him, Answerest thou nothing? what is it which these witness against thee? 63 But Jesus held his peace, And the high priest answered and said unto him, I adjure thee by the living God, that thou tell us whether thou be the Christ, the Son of God. 64 Jesus saith unto him, Thou hast said: nevertheless I say unto you, Hereafter shall ye see the Son of man sitting on the right hand of power, and coming in the clouds of heaven.	60 And the high priest stood up in the midst, and asked Jesus, saying, Answerest thou nothing? what is it which these witness against thee? 61 But he held his peace, and answered nothing. Again the high priest asked him, and said unto him, Art thou the Christ, the Son of the Blessed? 62 And Jesus said, I am: and ye shall see the Son of man sitting on the right hand of power, and coming in the clouds of heaven.	No Reference to the trial that took place inside Caiaphas' palace. Instead, Luke describes the manner they began to torture Jesus after that trial.	No Reference to the trial that took place in Caiaphas' palace or the trial with the Sanhedrin.

Examine 4 Gospels for Clues (KJV)

Matthew 26:65-66	Mark 14:63-64	Luke	John
65 Then the high priest rent his clothes, saying, He hath spoken blasphemy; what further need have we of witnesses? behold, now ye have heard his blasphemy. 66 What think ye? They answered and said, He is guilty of death.	63 Then the high priest rent his clothes, and saith, What need we any further witnesses? 64 Ye have heard the blasphemy: what think ye? And they all condemned him to be guilty of death.	No Reference to the trial that took place inside Caiaphas' palace. Instead, Luke describes the manner they began to torture Jesus after that trial.	No Reference to the trial that took place in Caiaphas' palace or the trial with the Sanhedrin.

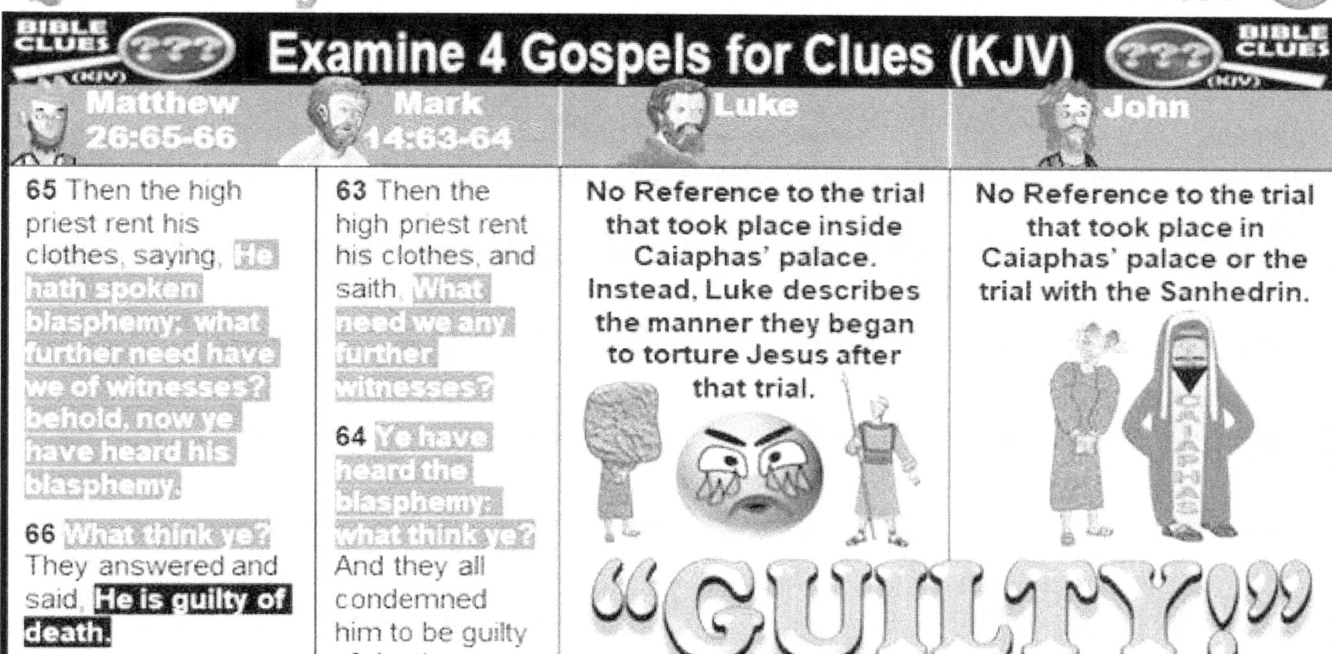

Jesus had to endure their false accusations, their torture, and Peter denying that he ever knew Him. He also had the dread of what was soon to happen.

Post 2ⁿᵈ Trial Torture of our Lord

Examine 4 Gospels for Clues (KJV)

Matthew 26:67-68	Mark 14:65	Luke 22:63-65	John
67 Then did they spit in his face, and buffeted him; and others smote him with the palms of their hands, 68 Saying, Prophesy unto us, thou Christ, Who is he that smote thee?	65 And some began to spit on him, and to cover his face, and to buffet him, and to say unto him, Prophesy; and the servants did strike him with the palms of their hands.	63 And the men that held Jesus mocked him, and smote him. 64 And when they had blindfolded him, they struck him on the face, and asked him, saying, Prophesy, who is it that smote thee? 65 And many other things blasphemously spake they against him.	No Reference to the trial that took place in Caiaphas' palace or the trial with the Sanhedrin.

GOOGLE DEFINITION: Buffet him means bodily maltreatment and violence and beat with the fist.

3RD OF 6 TRIALS FOR JESUS

3rd Trial for Jesus – Sanhedrin Trial

Examine 4 Gospels for Clues (KJV)

Matthew 27:1-2	Mark 15:1	Luke 22:66-67	John
1 When the morning was come, all the chief priests and elders of the people took counsel against Jesus to put him to death: **2** And when they had bound him, they led him away, and delivered him to Pontius Pilate the governor.	**1** And straightway in the morning the chief priests held a consultation with the elders and scribes and the whole council, and bound Jesus, and carried him away, and delivered him to Pilate.	**66** And as soon as it was day, the elders of the people and the chief priests and the scribes came together, and led him into their council, saying, **67** **Art thou the Christ? tell us.** …	No Reference to the trial that took place in Caiaphas' palace or the trial with the Sanhedrin.

Luke 22:67 … And he said unto them, If I tell you, ye will not believe: 68 And if I also ask you, ye will not answer me, nor let me go. 69 Hereafter shall the Son of man sit on the right hand of the power of God. (KJV)

Ye say that I am.

Luke 22: 66-71

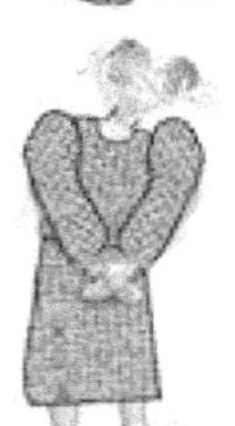

The first two trials held by the Sanhedrin transgressed their regulations. Why? According to Sanhedrin rules, no trials were allowed to be held in the dead of night; therefore, the trials held at the residences of Annas and Caiaphas were illegal.

The only legal trial was conducted the following morning at Sanhedrin Hall. But imagine this: If Jesus had been allowed to sleep at all, it would have been a very short sleep. Therefore, He would have been awake for more than 24 hours.

To conclude, Jesus would have been sleep-deprived and physically tortured for much of the night. He also had the agony of witnessing one of His twelve disciples betray Him; one denied Him three times, and the other ten scattered in various directions. Additionally, He had full awareness of what the next several hours would entail.

Please be aware that Jesus willingly went through all of this to save us from spending eternity in the Lake of Fire. He willingly suffered for our sakes. Will you accept His **FREE GIFT OF SALVATION**? With all my heart, I hope your answer is a grateful '**YES!**'

Have you ever faced the frustration of giving a truthful answer but not being believed? No matter what you said or how you defended yourself, the interrogator(s) was determined to only accept a lie as being the truth. That is what Jesus was facing with the Sanhedrin. Not for one second did they wish to entertain the concept that Jesus was indeed the Son of God nor the long-awaited Messiah. Therefore, in their closed-mindedness, they considered every word out of Jesus' mouth to be blasphemous.

Why did the Jewish elders in Bible days and even people today have such a hard time accepting the following truth about Jesus?

John 14:6 Jesus answered, "I am the way and the truth and the life. No one comes to the Father except through me." (NIV)

It requires them to willingly accept the challenge of making a **PARADIGM SHIFT**. Here is what that concept means:

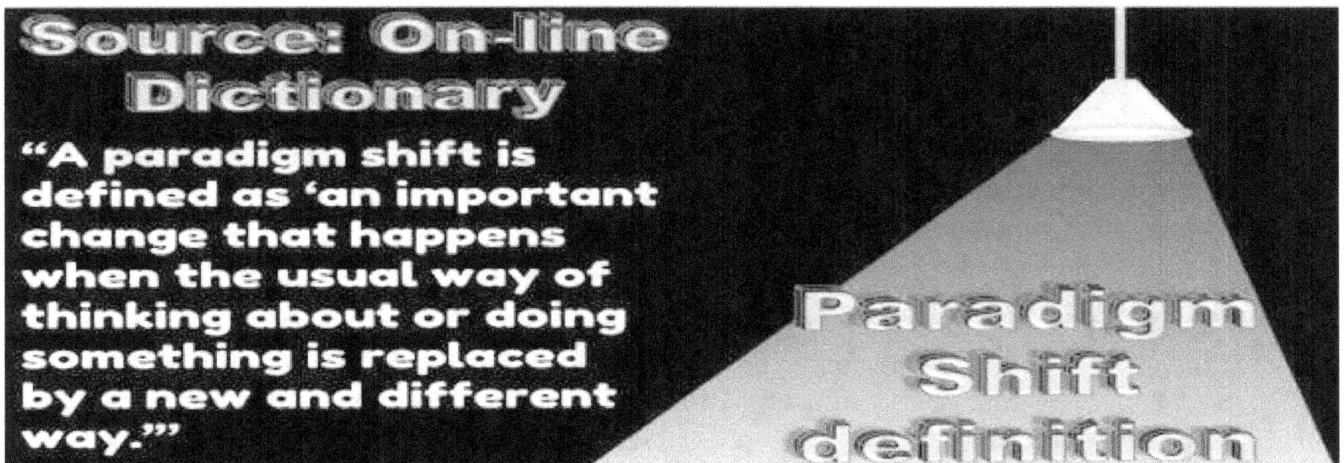

A classic example of a **PARADIGM SHIFT** is that many people believed the earth was flat before the voyages of Christopher Columbus, Ferdinand Magellan, and others. It took a lot of convincing for them to make the **PARADIGM SHIFT** to be accepting, some by faith alone, that the earth was round or spherical.

To her peril, Eve and her husband Adam made the **PARADIGM SHIFT** of believing they would die if they tasted the fruit from the Tree of the Knowledge of Good and Evil to allow the Serpent to entice them into believing this narrative was false. After tasting the fruit, their physical bodies didn't die, but their easy lives in the Garden of Eden did. From that time forward, they had to live a more challenging and tumultuous life on Earth. (**Genesis 3:1-24**)

Noah also had to make a **PARADIGM SHIFT**. He started building the Ark on faith alone at the age of 500. Noah had to wait 100 years for this predicted flood to take place. Despite enduring people's doubts and ridicule, Noah persevered and received the ultimate reward: Life for himself and his family, while death came for all other humans on earth.

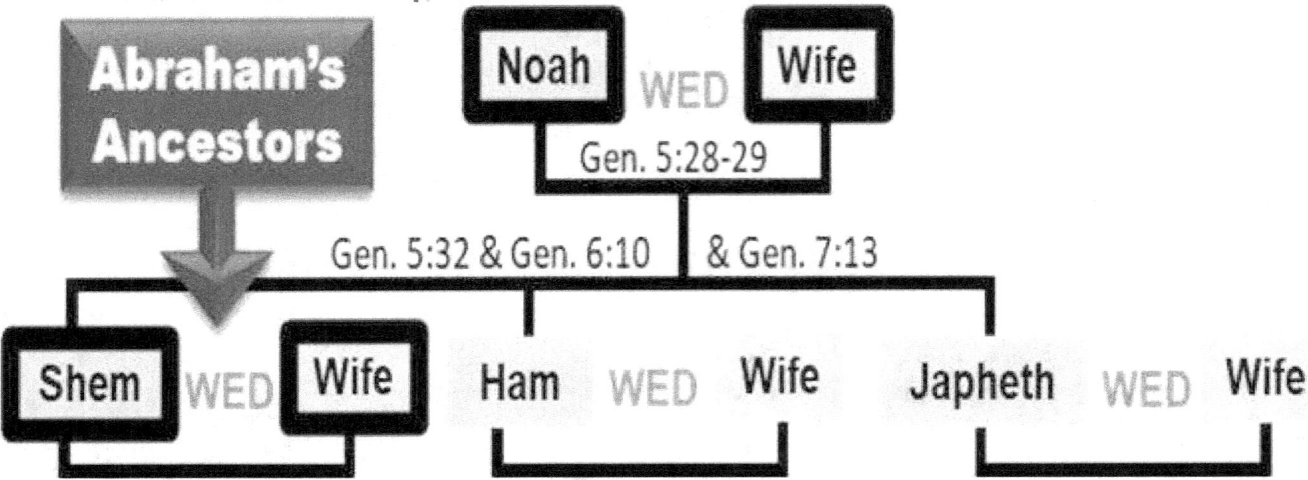

Just think of how many **PARADIGM SHIFTS** Moses had to endure in his lifetime. Unknown to him, he was born to a Hebrew woman in captivity, destined to be murdered along with all other baby boys during that period. Then, at about three months old, he became the pampered adoptive son of the Egyptian Pharoah's daughter. Years later, in defense of a Hebrew enslaved person, he murdered an Egyptian overseer. So, his next shift was being a convict on the run for his life. He married, had two sons, and lived as a shepherd, working for his father-in-law. The next thing he knew, God (i.e., Yahweh) spoke to Moses by way of a burning bush. This sent him on his next shift to convince the current Pharoah, his former foster brother, to let his Hebrew people go. The story goes on from there. (**Exodus 2 to 12 and beyond**)

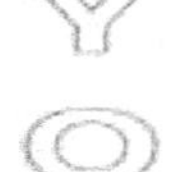

Think about your **PARADIGM SHIFTS**. You were a baby, toddler, child, preteen, teenager, young adult, etc. Among the many hats you wear or have worn, you might have identified as the following: Husband, wife, significant other, sibling, parent, employee, boss, Christian, non-Christian, introvert, extrovert, etc. You may also identify yourself as a particular race or culture.

Using the Jewish calendar and rounding a birth year up or down by mid-century time spans, here is the beginning of a timeline shown in its entirety later in this book.

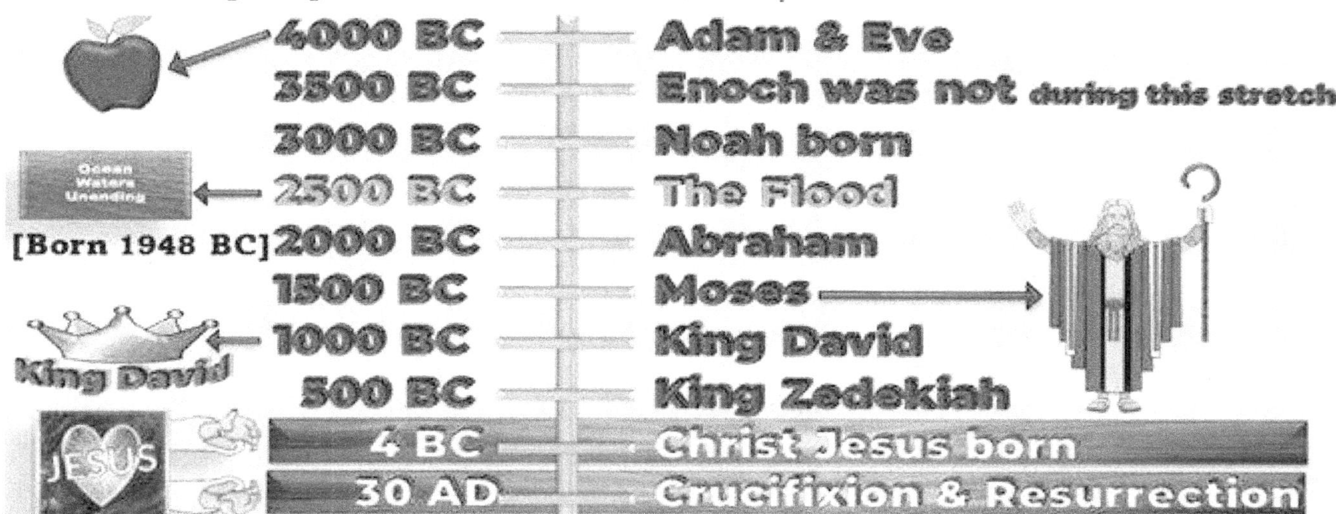

In **John 8:56-58**, Jesus asked the Jewish people to make an extreme **PARADIGM SHIFT**. He asked them to believe that He existed 2000 years before Abraham was even born. Jesus said the following:

> **John 8:58 "Very truly I tell you," Jesus answered, "before Abraham was born, I am!" (NIV)**

Jesus' phraseology was likely extra incendiary due to what the Jewish elders knew and accepted that God had said to Moses about five hundred years after Abraham was born and fifteen hundred years before Jesus was born:

> **Exodus 3:13 Moses said to God, "Suppose I go to the Israelites and say to them, 'The God of your fathers has sent me to you,' and they ask me, 'What is his name?' Then what shall I tell them?"**
>
> **Exodus 3:14 God said to Moses, "I am who I am. This is what you are to say to the Israelites: 'I am has sent me to you.'" (NIV)**

The Israelites and Jewish elders had very boxed-in views of what type of man would match their criteria for being the long-awaited Messiah. Due to their stubborn nature and lack of willingness to change, they did not want to make the **PARADIGM SHIFT** of accepting Jesus to be that man.

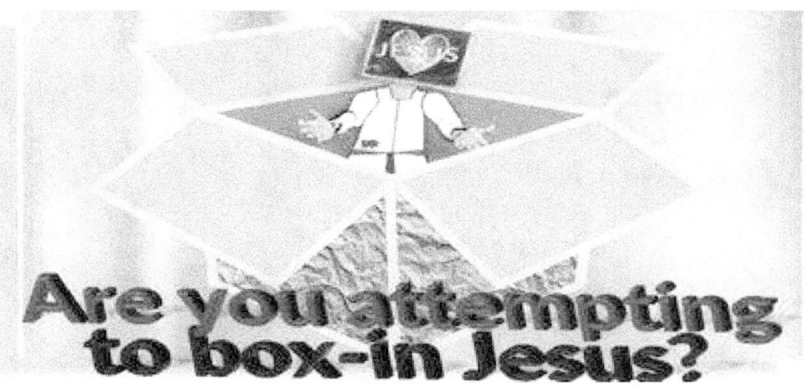

About six months before Jesus was crucified, He secretly attended the fall annual 8-day Feast of Tabernacles that begins and ends on the Sabbath. Only at the halfway point did the Pharisees discover Jesus teaching in the courtyard of the Jerusalem Temple. Why did He have to attend in secret? Jesus was aware that the Pharisees sought to kill Him, but it was not yet the previously decided-upon time. (**John 7:1** through **John 8:59**)

When Jesus made that statement about Abraham, the Pharisees wished to stone Him as they wanted this unwanted messenger eliminated. Six months later, during Passover Seder, the Pharisees thought they finally got their wish.

So, what other **PARADIGM SHIFTS** was Jesus trying to help the Jewish people make? I had to watch several Feast of Tabernacle YouTube videos to give me context clues. Understanding how the Jews organized this festival during the time of Jesus helped give me a deeper understanding of the tremendous benefits of being a follower of Christ.

> **Leviticus 23:33 The Lord said to Moses, 34 "Say to the Israelites: 'On the fifteenth day of the seventh month the Lord's Festival of Tabernacles begins, and it lasts for seven days.**
>
> **THIS USUALLY HAPPENS IN SEPTEMBER OR OCTOBER CELEBRATING THAT YEAR'S GOD-PROVIDED SUCCESSFUL HARVEST. IT MIGHT BE CONSIDERED TO BE SLIGHTLY SIMILAR TO THE UNITED STATES HOLIDAY CALLED THANKSGIVING.**
>
> **Leviticus 23:35 The first day is a sacred assembly; do no regular work. 36 For seven days present food offerings to the Lord, and on the eighth day hold a sacred assembly and present a food offering to the Lord. It is the closing special assembly; do no regular work. (NIV)**

Here is an example of a **Sukkah Booth or Tent** temporarily constructed for this festival:

Leviticus 23:42 "Live in temporary shelters for seven days: All native-born Israelites are to live in such shelters 43 so your descendants will know that I had the Israelites live in temporary shelters when I brought them out of Egypt. I am the Lord your God.'" (NIV)

You have seen an example of a Sukkah tent. They would eat this type of food.

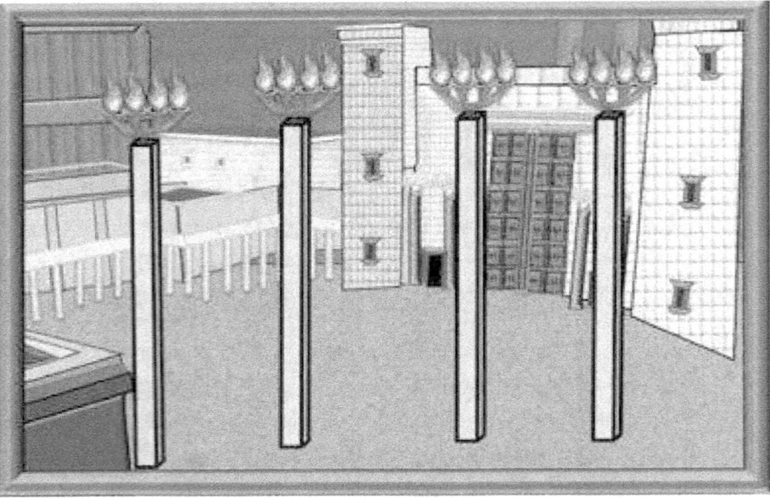

As you can see from the picture, four 75-foot-tall lampstands towered over the Court of the Women. Each lamp consisted of four bowls filled with olive oil. Each afternoon of the 8-day festival, the people would come to observe four agile priests climbing to the top of the lampstand to light each oil lamp. That might be similar to us watching trapeze artists or tightrope walkers in modern-day circuses. Their mouths were probably hanging open in wonder and amazement.

Now, imagine yourself back in the days before electricity had been invented. After dark, you would require a lantern or candle if you wandered through your house or place of employment. You must carry a lit torch or lantern if you wandered around your town or city. Even so, there would be many dark shadows and disturbing night noises.

It must have been so rewarding to be able to stare outside your Sukkah booth to see the courtyards of Jerusalem lit up in such a bright manner. It would certainly be conducive to meditating about the Children of Israel, led by Moses, wandering the wilderness for 40 years.

Exodus 13:21 And the Lord went before them by day in a pillar of a cloud, to lead them the way; and by night in a pillar of fire, to give them light; to go by day and night: 22 He took not away the pillar of the cloud by day, nor the pillar of fire by night, from before the people. (KJV)

Jewish Roots.net called this ceremony the "**Illumination of the Temple**" and confirmed its purpose was "*to remind the people of the pillar of fire that had guided Israel in their wilderness journey.*"

Israel My Glory.org gave this additional explanation. "*The illumination from these imposing Temple lamps symbolized two realities. The first was the reality of the "Light of all Lights"— the "Shekinah Glory—the visible presence of God" that filled the first Temple, which Solomon built (**1 Kings 8:10–11**). The second was Ha or Gadol (**the Great Light**) who would soon come and bring light to those who were spiritually dead and dwelling in darkness (**Isaiah. 9:2**).*"

With this awareness in mind, the people might have been ripe to make the necessary **PARADIGM SHIFT** when they heard Jesus speak on this festival's 8th and final day. In John 8:12, John explained what happened on that day when Jesus shared these profound words.

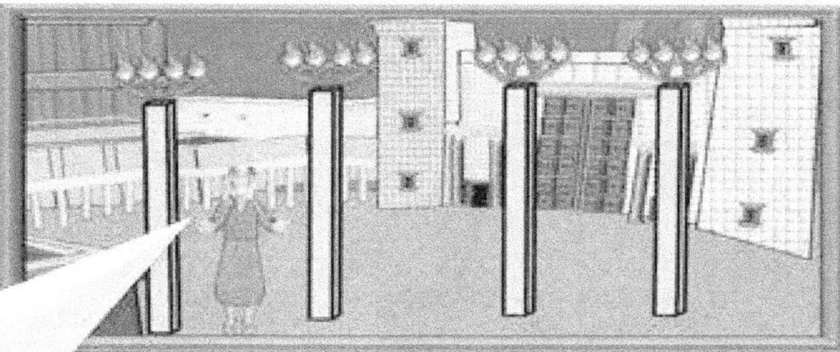

There were some other **PARADIGM SHIFTS** Jesus asked His listeners to make regarding the issue of light. See the images below:

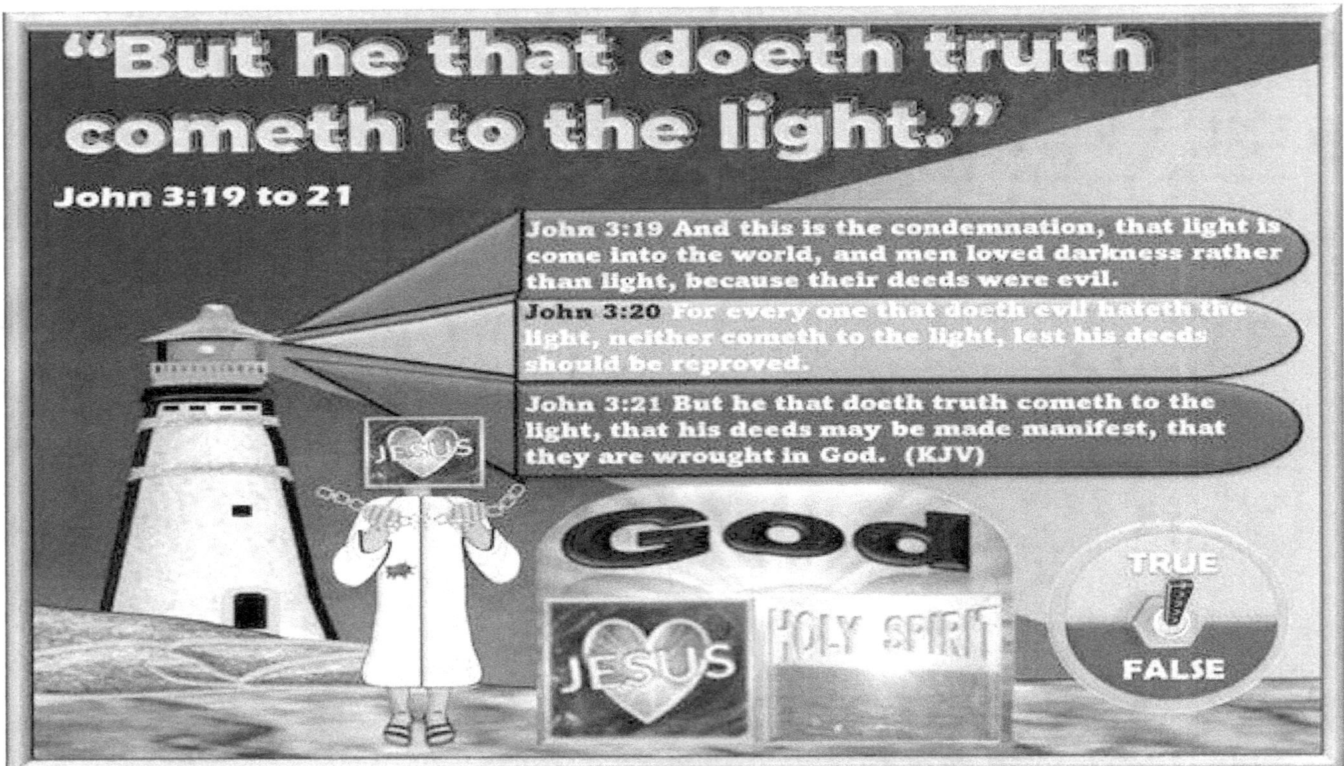

But Jesus did not want His listeners to only think about Him being the light. He wanted to give a **CALL TO ACTION** so they knew they had a duty to fulfill in their own right. This actionable step is just as accurate today, if not to a greater degree than it was during the first century AD.

On this eighth and final day of the festival, Jesus was also concerned that a man who had never been able to see the light of day would receive healing, even if it happened to be the Sabbath. As you may recall, this eight-day festival began and ended on the Sabbath.

Jesus and His Disciples saw a blind man begging. He had been blind from the day he was born. It was likely that the Disciples believed that his blindness was due to generational sin. So, in **John 9:2**, one of His Disciples asked:

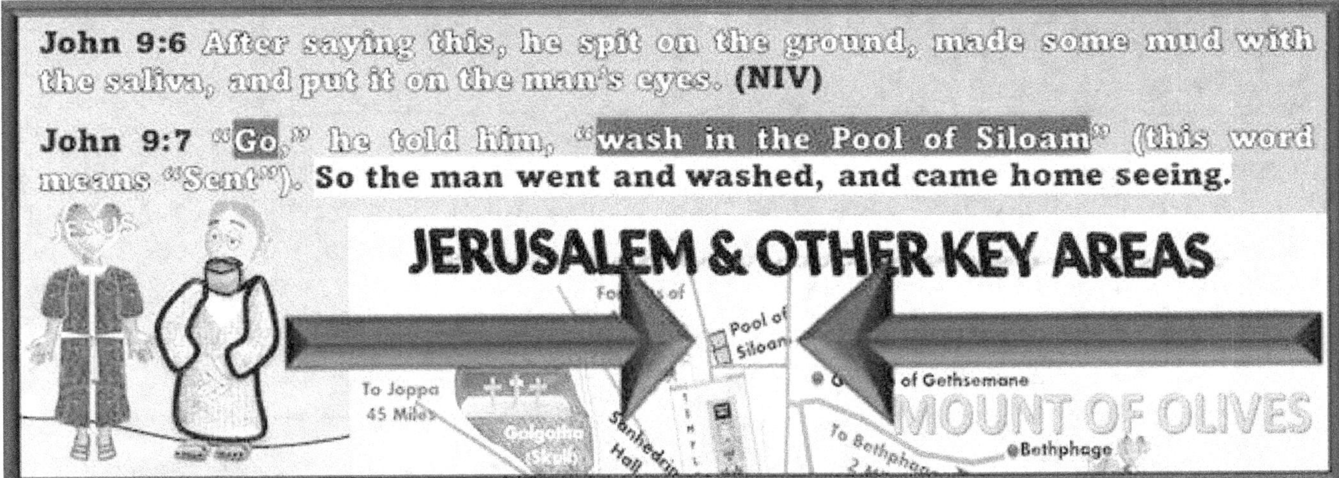

John 9:6 After saying this, he spit on the ground, made some mud with the saliva, and put it on the man's eyes. **(NIV)**

John 9:7 "Go," he told him, "wash in the Pool of Siloam" (this word means "Sent"). So the man went and washed, and came home seeing.

Naturally, this incident caused quite the stir.

John 9:8 **His neighbors and those who had formerly seen him begging asked,** "Isn't this the same man who used to sit and beg?"

John 9:9 **Some claimed that he was. Others said,** "No, he only looks like him." **But he himself insisted, "I am the man."**

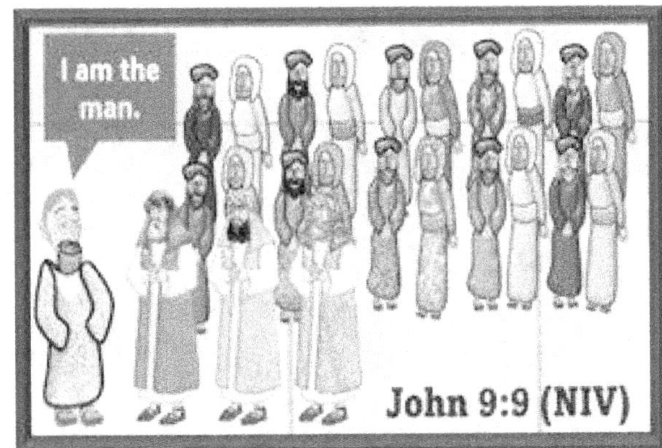

John 9:10 "How then were your eyes opened?" they asked.   (NIV)

John 9:11 He replied, "The man they call Jesus made some mud and put it on my eyes. He told me to go to Siloam and wash. So I went and washed, and then I could see."

John 9:12 "Where is this man?" they asked him. "I don't know," he said.

As you can well imagine, the Pharisees were in an uproar. Jesus had the audacity to heal somebody on the Sabbath! How dare he! They called in the formerly blind man to listen to his testimony. The Pharisees were divided in their opinions.

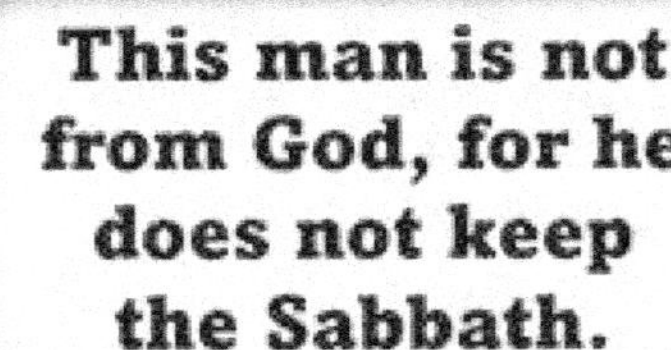

A Pharisee turned to the formerly blind man and asked:

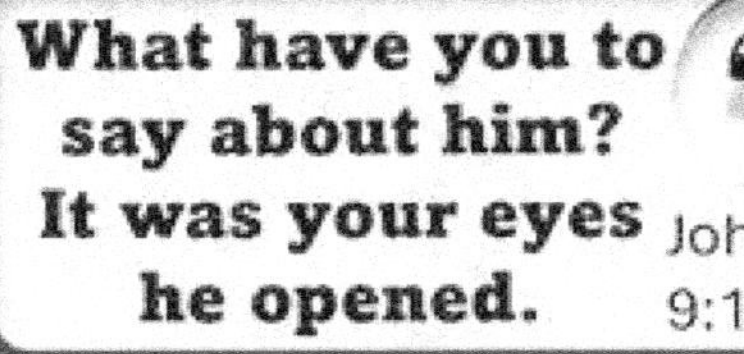

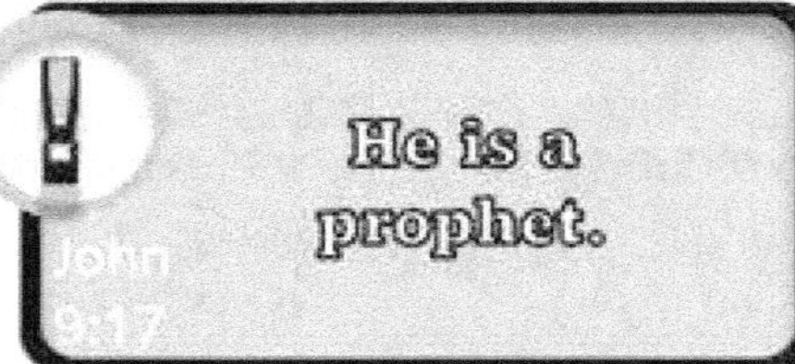

Suspecting this was '*fake news*,' as we often hear that term used today, they called in the parents of this formerly blind man. We learn in **John 9:20-23** that the parents confirmed the man was their son and that he had been blind from birth. But fearing the Pharisees would excommunicate them from the Temple, they wisely stated, "**Ask him. He is of age; he will speak for himself.**"

They called the formerly blind man back to the temple and demanded:

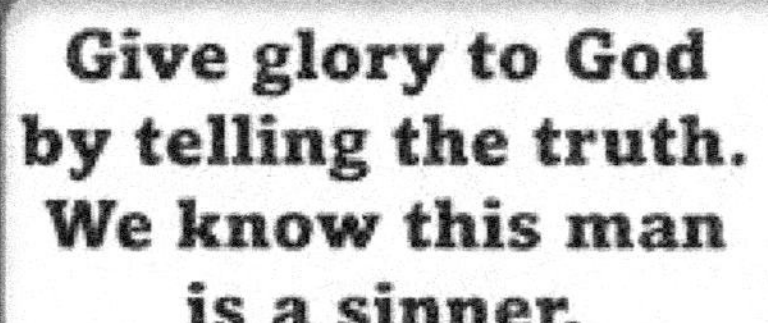

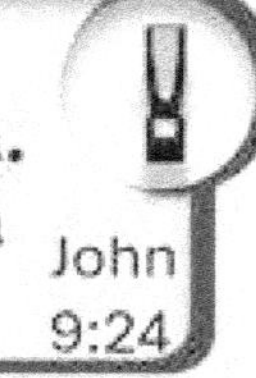

Still not getting the expected answers, they questioned him a second time.

Infuriated, the Pharisees insulted him. Then, they proudly exclaimed:

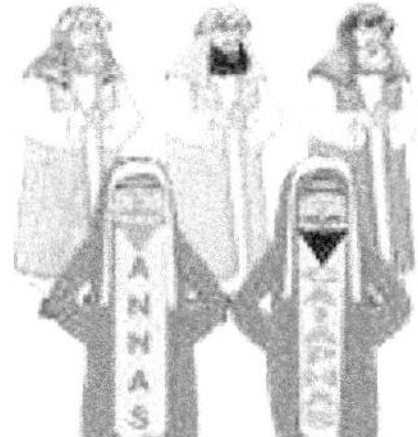

In **John 9:34**, we learn that the proud and arrogant Pharisees were incensed. They threw the formerly blind man out of the Temple.

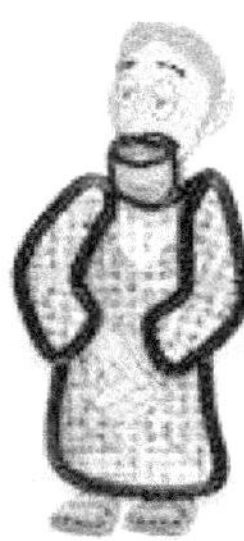

The Bible's New International Version **(NIV)** gives the title of 'Spiritual Blindness' to the interaction between Jesus and the Pharisees (John 9:35-41). So, in case that last verse felt jarring to you, just as it likely did to the Pharisee who had to listen to Jesus' accusing words, I felt inspired to learn more. I wanted to comprehend what it means to be spiritually blind within the context of those times. I also wanted to take inventory of my own life and interactions to ensure that I am not guilty of those transgressions. I want nothing to separate me from Jesus in any way. You may want to do this about your life interactions, as well.

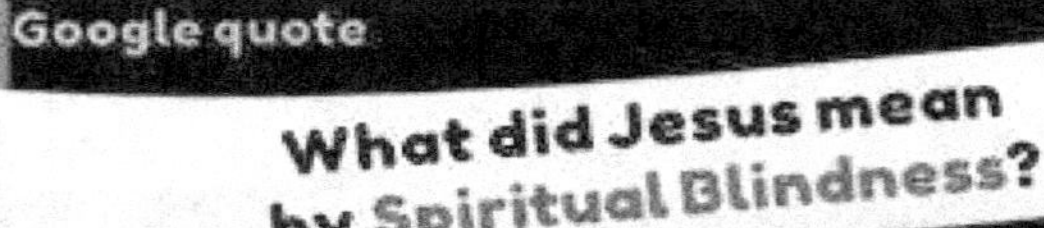
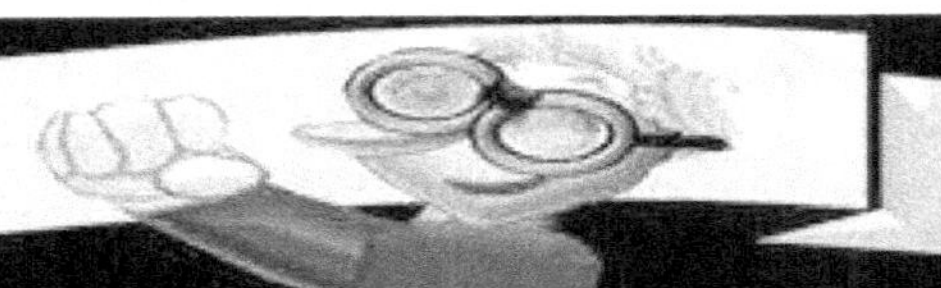

That situation brings to mind an idiom, where one 'can't see the forest for the trees'. Cambridge Dictionary (dictionary.cambridge.org) defines this as "to be unable to understand a situation clearly because you are too involved in it."

These photos were taken on one of my former trips to Icy Point Strait, Alaska.

The Pharisees were so caught up in legalism and rigidly following each rule of their spiritual practice that they were not willing to see the bigger picture. Instead of celebrating that a man who had been blind from birth could now see, they were doubly incensed that this healing occurred from a man they had not vetted or authorized and that it happened on the Sabbath.

The **PARADIGM SHIFT** Jesus longed for them to make was to follow their rules and the 10 Commandments still but to also more fully embrace His 2 Commandments to fully Love God and Agape Love all humankind.

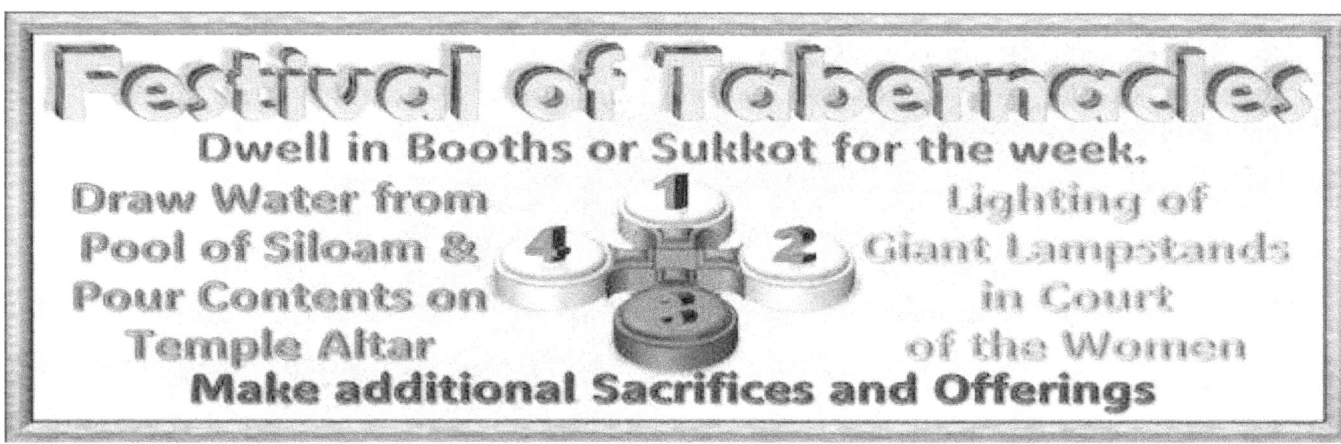

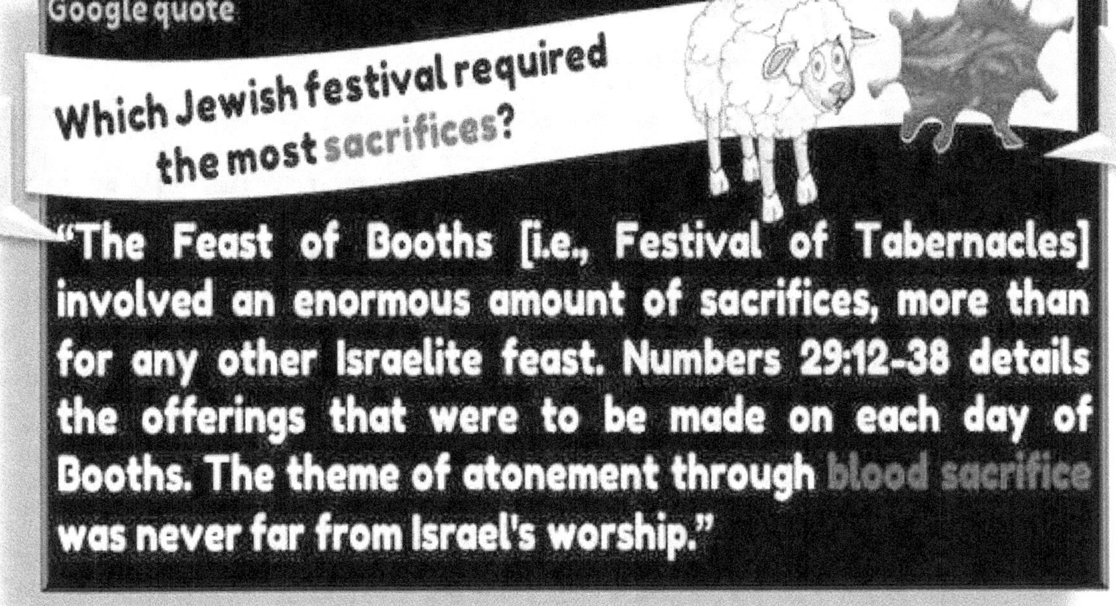

During the Festival of Tabernacles, also called the Feast of Booths, among other names, the priests made multiple animal sacrifices to free the Jews from their sinful natures. Read **Numbers 29:12-40** below for a complete description.

Day 1 of 8

Numbers 29:12 "'On the fifteenth day of the seventh month, hold a sacred assembly and do no regular work. Celebrate a festival to the Lord for seven days. 13 Present as an aroma pleasing to the Lord a food offering consisting of a burnt offering of thirteen young bulls, two rams and fourteen male lambs a year old, all without defect. 14 With each of the thirteen bulls offer a grain offering of three-tenths of an ephah of the finest flour mixed with oil; with each of the two rams, two-tenths; 15 and with each of the fourteen lambs, one-tenth. 16 Include one male goat as a sin offering, in addition to the regular burnt offering with its grain offering and drink offering. (NIV)

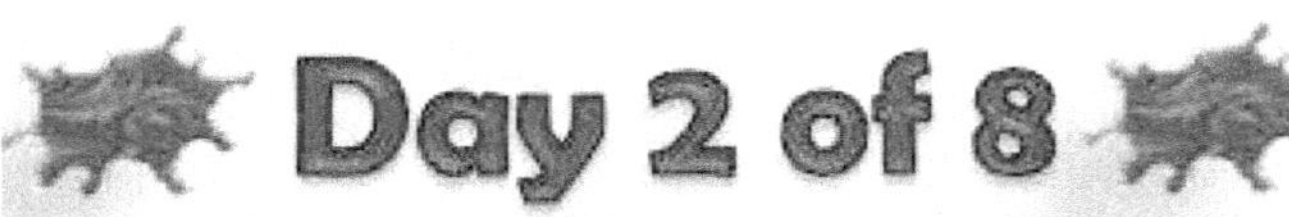

Day 2 of 8

Numbers 29:17 "'On the second day offer twelve young bulls, two rams and fourteen male lambs a year old, all without defect. 18 With the bulls, rams and lambs, offer their grain offerings and drink offerings according to the number specified. 19 Include one male goat as a sin offering, in addition to the regular burnt offering with its grain offering, and their drink offerings. (NIV)

Day 3 of 8

Numbers 29:20 "'On the third day offer eleven bulls, two rams and fourteen male lambs a year old, all without defect. 21 With the bulls, rams and lambs, offer their grain offerings and drink offerings according to the number specified. 22 Include one male goat as a sin offering, in addition to the regular burnt offering with its grain offering and drink offering. (NIV)

Day 4 of 8

Numbers 29:23 "'On the fourth day offer ten bulls, two rams and fourteen male lambs a year old, all without defect. 24 With the bulls, rams and lambs, offer their grain offerings and drink offerings according to the number specified. 25 Include one male goat as a sin offering, in addition to the regular burnt offering with its grain offering and drink offering. (NIV)

Day 5 of 8

Numbers 29:26 "'On the **fifth day** offer nine bulls, two rams and fourteen male lambs a year old, all without defect. 27 With the bulls, rams and lambs, offer their grain offerings and drink offerings according to the number specified. 28 Include one male goat as a sin offering, in addition to the 2regular burnt offering with its grain offering and drink offering. (NIV)

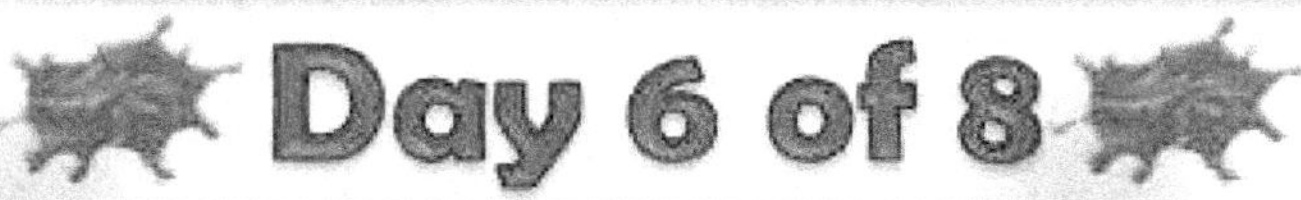

Day 6 of 8

Numbers 29:29 "'On the **sixth day** offer eight bulls, two rams and fourteen male lambs a year old, all without defect. 30 With the bulls, rams and lambs, offer their grain offerings and drink offerings according to the number specified. 31 Include one male goat as a sin offering, in addition to the regular burnt offering with its grain offering and drink offering. (NIV)

Day 7 of 8

Numbers 29:32 "'On the **seventh day** offer seven bulls, two rams and fourteen male lambs a year old, all without defect. 33 With the bulls, rams and lambs, offer their grain offerings and drink offerings according to the number specified. 34 Include one male goat as a sin offering, in addition to the regular burnt offering with its grain offering and drink offering. (NIV)

Day 8 of 8

Numbers 29:35 "'On the **eighth day** hold a closing special assembly and do no regular work. 36 Present as an aroma pleasing to the Lord a food offering consisting of a burnt offering of one bull, one ram and seven male lambs a year old, all without defect. 37 With the bull, the ram and the lambs, offer their grain offerings and drink offerings according to the number specified. 38 Include one male goat as a sin offering, in addition to the regular burnt offering with its grain offering and drink offering. (NIV)

Numbers 29:39 "'In addition to what you vow and your freewill offerings, offer these to the Lord at your appointed festivals: your burnt offerings, grain offerings, drink offerings and fellowship offerings.'"

Numbers 29:40 **Moses told the Israelites all that the Lord commanded him.** (NIV)

The sounds and smells of those multiple sacrifices must have permeated the whole city of Jerusalem. The Jewish people were likely thanking God that there was a relatively easy way (unless you were one of those animals) to be freed from God's judgment for the sins they had committed in the previous year. They must have also been aware that this would have to occur each year of their lives if they wanted God to welcome them into Heaven. If only there were an easier way! Then, along came Jesus, who said:

John 8:51 **Verily, verily, I say unto you, If a man keep my saying, he shall never see death**. (KJV)

The Amplified Bible described Jesus' statement in this manner:

John 8:51 **I assure you and most solemnly say to you, if anyone keeps My word** [by living in accordance with My message] **he will indeed never, ever see and experience death** [i.e., spiritual death and separation from God.]."

If you are already a Christian, then I am preaching to the choir. But if you have not yet accepted Christ as your Lord and Savior, do you comprehend what an extraordinary offer is currently being made to you – for **FREE**? You do not have to pay money or bribes to get this. It is **FREE**!

You may think, "**But you do not know the amounts of sins or the type of sins I have committed. There is no way that Jesus would be willing to accept me!**"

If you have yet to read the New Testament, Jesus spent most of His time hanging out with people who had sinned in all manner of iniquities. He did not love the sins they committed, but He sincerely **Agape LOVED** them all.

With Jesus, it is genuinely a COME AS YOU ARE PARTY. He will meet you right where you are currently located. This includes His younger brothers and sisters who are serving terms of incarceration. He does not consider even one of us a lost cause. Even if you accidentally or purposely made a pact with the devil. The Blood of Jesus and the Holy Spirit can break those chains. You can even Google available Deliverance Ministries should you need extra help to be set free.

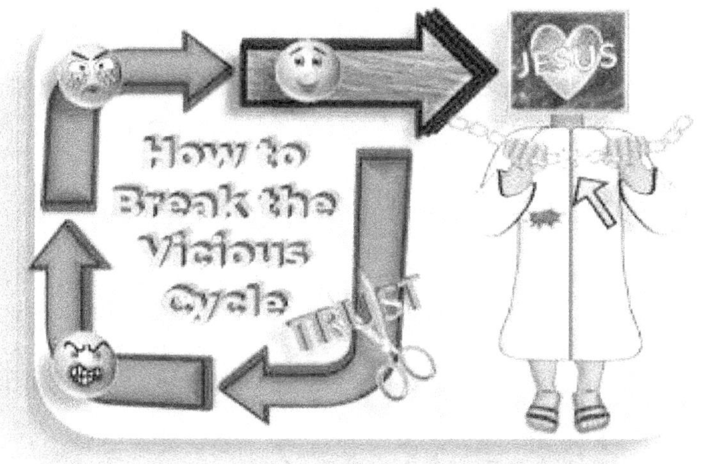

Ephesians 6:10 Finally, my brethren, be strong in the Lord, and in the power of his might. 11 Put on the whole armor of God, that ye may be able to stand against the wiles of the devil.

12 For we wrestle not against flesh and blood, but against principalities, against powers, against the rulers of the darkness of this world, against spiritual wickedness in high places.

13 Wherefore take unto you the whole armor of God, that ye may be able to withstand in the evil day, and having done all, to stand. (KJV)

God formed each of us in our mother's womb, intending for us to accomplish many things for Him.

Jeremiah 29:11 "For I know the plans I have for you," declares the Lord, "plans to prosper you and not to harm you, plans to give you hope and a future." (NIV Bible)

The Triune God: Father God, Lord Jesus, and the Holy Spirit LOVES each of us with more Love than we can imagine. You may have heard this song and even criticized it for its simplicity. But ponder the lyrics written in the late 1800s by a Chicago, Illinois preacher, Clarence Herbert Woolston (1856-1927). He was likely inspired by reading **Matthew 19:13-14** and **Mark 10:13-16**.

Jesus Loves the Little Children

Lyrics by Clarence Herbert Woolston (1856-1927)

Jesus loves the little children - All the children of the world

Red and yellow, black and white. They are precious in His sight

Jesus loves the little children of the world

Jesus died for all the children - All the children of the world

Red and yellow, black and white. They are precious in His sight

Jesus died for all the children of the world

Let me ask you this. Would the devil step up and die in your place? Would any other prophet, voodoo priest or priestess, witch or warlock, or Satanic leader you may revere or worship volunteer to lay down his or her life on your behalf? NO! But Jesus willingly allowed Himself to be painfully slaughtered for us!

Contrary to what you may think, Satan does not rule hell. God created the Lake of Fire to throw Satan and the Fallen Angels into upon Jesus' Second Coming.

Satan and his demons hate our guts because God created us in His image and likeness. I recently listened to a YouTube video about a Man of God who regularly conducts Deliverance Ministries. As he extracted a demon from a person desperate to be saved, he asked the demon why he allowed Lucifer to convince him to leave Heaven. The demon bitterly admitted that Lucifer had made all kinds of big promises to a third of God's Angels that never saw fruition. Lucifer was originally beautiful and very convincing, so these Fallen Angels, now ugly demons, fell for those lies. So, there is no way to escape their eventual fate. Satan even tortures them if they do not entrap as many humans as possible to help populate their future prison.

In like manner, Satan may have promised you fame and fortune. You may even be living a life of luxury and popularity. But on the day you take your last breath and close your eyes on this life, you will awaken to find yourself in a raging hot solitary cell in hell, being tortured 24/7, with nothing to eat or drink, no drugs or alcohol, no cigarettes or vaping or pot, no music, no entertainment, no friendship, no parties, and never being allowed to sleep or rest or bleed or die. You will have to smell the most putrid smells. Several NDErs said they could not even discern whether the hideous bodies they saw being tortured by demons and then put together again, only to be torn apart again and again, were male or female. Remember, if you do not repent and choose God, then:

John 8:44 You belong to your father, the devil, and you want to carry out your father's desires. He was a murderer from the beginning, not holding to the truth, for there is no truth in him. When he lies, he speaks his native language, for he is a liar and the father of lies. (NIV)

Jesus is heartbroken when any of us choose to precede or follow Satan into hell. The Triune God was so desperate to save us from the fate intended exclusively for Lucifer and the Fallen Angels that they were willing to send Jesus to live on this earth for about 33 years to take our place on the Cross. You may say, "Well, if they feel like that, why do they send people to that horrible place?"

Jesus is a gentleman. He does not want us to become a robot or a 'Stepford wife.' He wants our love and reverence but will not force us to love Him. We can use our **FREE WILL** to choose to honor and follow Jesus or cater to the devil.

Ever since Jesus was crucified, resurrected, and ascended to Heaven, accepting Him as your Lord and Savior is the **ONLY** way God will wipe you clean of your sins. Here is one of the many versions of a **SINNER'S PRAYER** you could choose to pray to be saved and redeemed by Jesus:

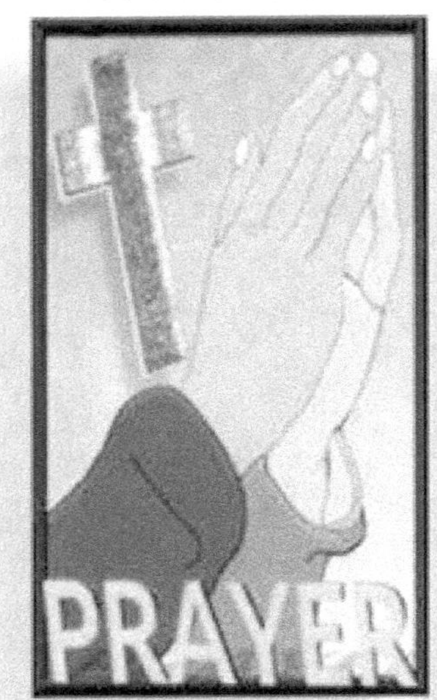

Dear Lord Jesus, I know that I am a sinner, and I ask for Your forgiveness. I believe You died for my sins and rose from the dead. I turn from my sins and invite You to come into my heart and life. I want to trust and follow You as my Lord and Savior. -- GOOGLE QUOTE

Don't delay, as the Tribulation is likely to happen very soon. If you take the **MARK OF THE BEAST from the Antichrist** or **die prematurely** in a car wreck or from an illness of some type and have not chosen to accept Christ, then hell will be your destination. But if you sincerely choose Christ, and He can read your thoughts and your heart, then you will be able to legally PLEAD THE BLOOD OF JESUS and be saved from hell. The choice is up to you. Please, please, please choose Jesus, as we don't want you to spend eternity in hell.

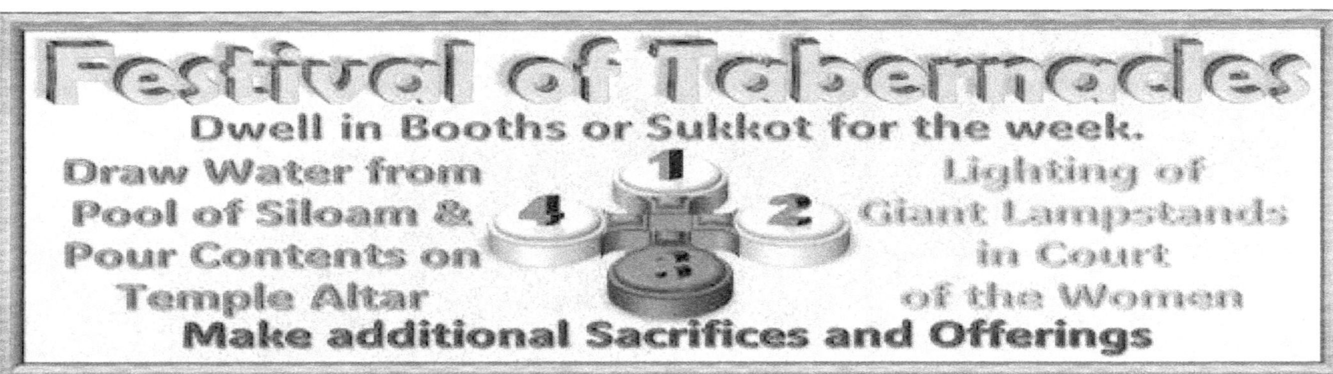

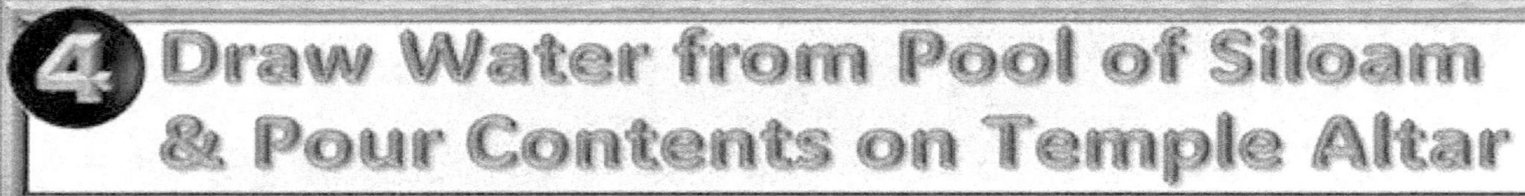

Imagine this. On the morning of the festival's first day, a priest would blow a ram's horn called a **SHOFAR**. That was the official notice that the **Festival of the Tabernacles** had begun.

Priests would come out of the Temple. Excited Israelites would exit their Sukkah Booths. A few would play some music that included a flute.

What was their destination? They were heading for Jerusalem's only clean water source at the Pool of Siloam. The water in this pool originated from the Gihon Spring. Because this pool was a spring-fed water source, the Jews called it **LIVING WATER**.

At the head of the procession was a priest carrying a golden pitcher. He aimed to plunge his pitcher into the pool to draw out some of this **LIVING WATER**. As he did this, he recited a verse from **Isaiah 12:3** that stated:

Isaiah 12:3 "Therefore with joy shall ye draw water out of the wells of salvation." (KJV)

Israel My Glory.org gives us two remarkable pieces of information.*

1 *"Accompanying the chant was the sweet sound of an instrument called the reed flute of Moses.* Moses means "to draw out." *(Pharoah's daughter named him that because she drew him out of the water [Ex. 2:10].)"*

2 *"When people asked why the ritual was called "*the drawing out of water*," they were told, "because of the pouring out of the Ruach Ha-Kodesh [Holy Spirit]."* The water symbolized the Holy Spirit, the only true source of life.*

The next step was for the priest to carry this LIVING WATER back to the Temple. Another priest, carrying a goblet of wine, joined him.

The trumpet blower would blow his **Shofar** three times.

The two priests would go up the ramp inside the Temple, approach the Great Altar, and pour both liquids into a specified silver funnel.

In the meantime, the rest of the people would gather at the Court of the Women. There would be people singing songs originating from **Psalm 113 to 118**. Others would play instruments. People would be expressing gratitude.

Picture this court packed with hundreds of excited people.

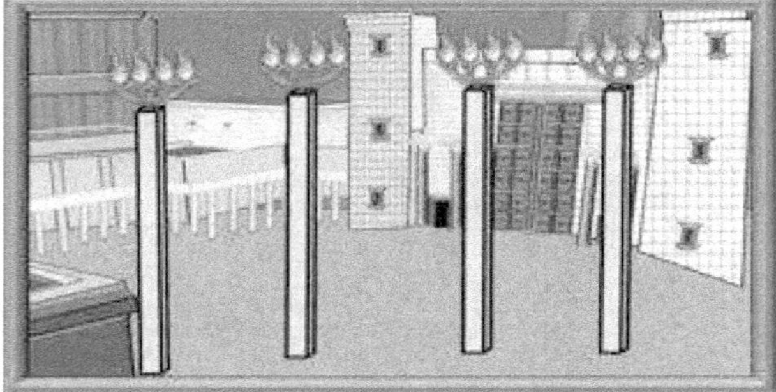

In the meantime, there would be a procession of priests holding willow branches, who would march around the Great Altar once. Then, the people would listen as the priests called out words from **Psalm 118:25**.

> **Psalm 118:25 "Save now, I beseech thee, O Lord: O Lord, I beseech thee, send now prosperity." (KJV)**

There would then be moments of silence as people inwardly thanked God for providing them with rains that fed their harvests from the previous year. They would also request God to send them the appropriate amount of rain to feed their next year's harvest.

This ceremony was repeated each morning from the second day of the eight-day festival to the seventh day. On the seventh day, the priests would march around the Great Altar seven times instead of just once. Israel My Glory.org explained, "This last day of the Feast was Hoshanah Rabbah (the Great Praise Day)."

If people weren't excited enough, in **John 7:37-44**, we learn that Jesus did something extraordinary.

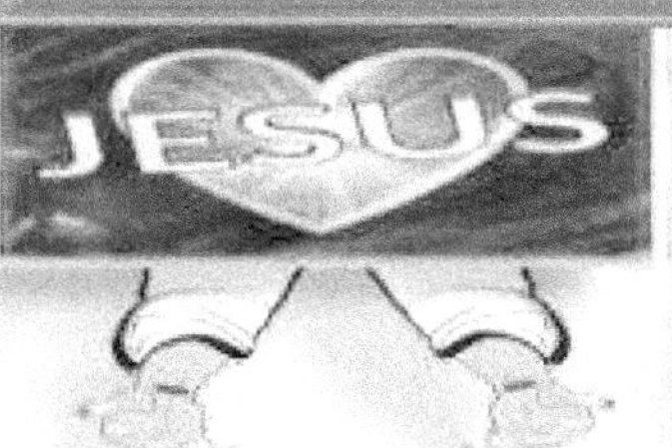

John 7:39 (But this spake he of the Spirit, which they that believe on him should receive: for the Holy Ghost was not yet given; because that Jesus was not yet glorified.)

John 7:40 Many of the people therefore, when they heard this saying, said, Of a truth this is the Prophet. 41 Others said, This is the Christ. But some said, Shall Christ come out of Galilee? 42 Hath not the scripture said, That Christ cometh of the seed of David, and out of the town of Bethlehem, where David was?

John 7:43 So there was a division among the people because of him.

John 7:44 And some of them would have taken him; but no man laid hands on him. (KJV)

Some amazing things happened during this festival. As stated previously, this took place about six months before the Crucifixion. At this event, Jesus openly admitted His true identity to anyone who would listen. Some believed Him. Some were unwilling to entertain such a notion. Others needed to figure out what to believe or disbelieve.

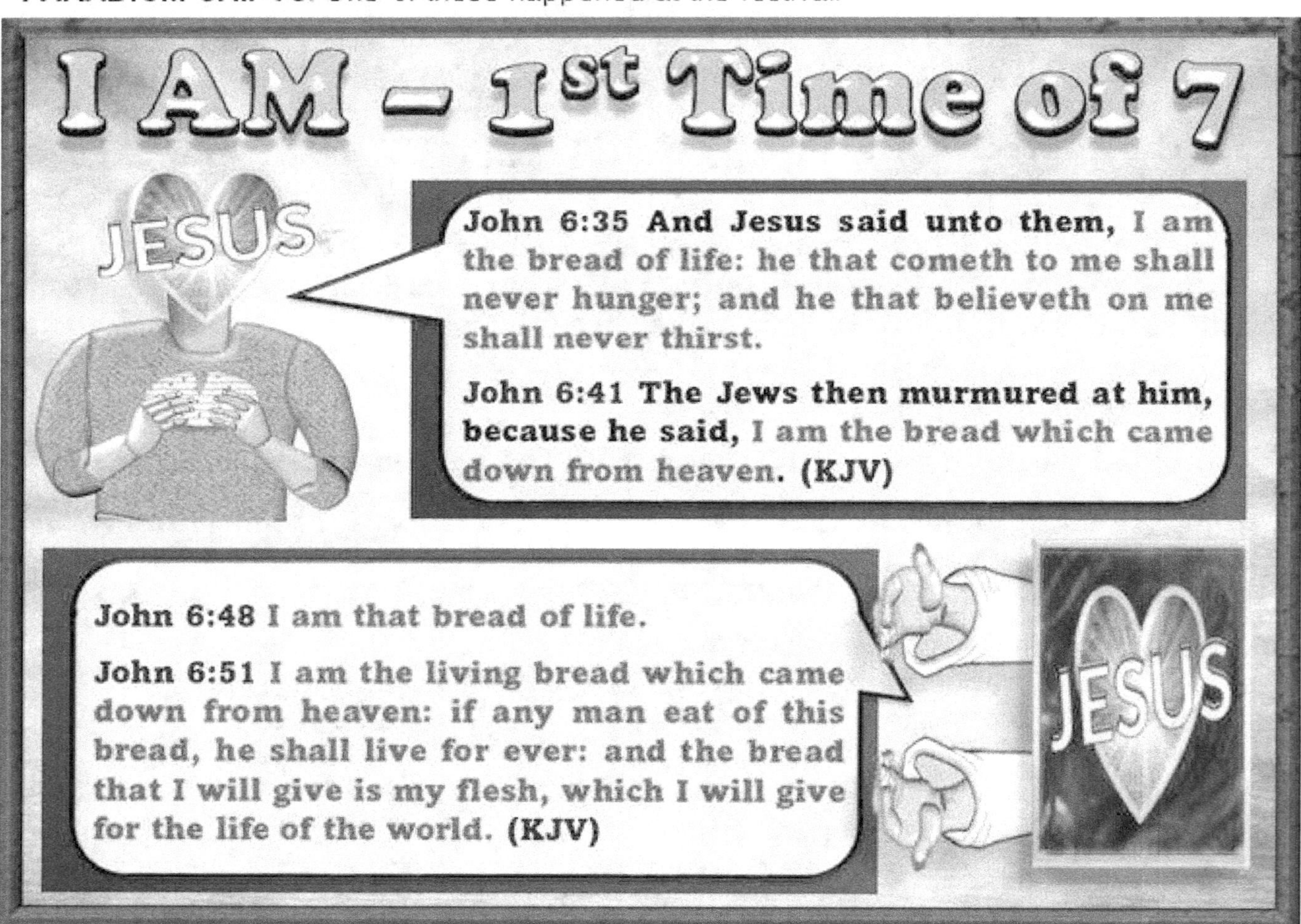

The book of John spelled out more details about Jesus' divinity. For example, I was introduced to the idea, through Got Question.org, that "*Jesus used the same phrase I AM' in seven declarations about Himself. In all seven, He combines I AM with tremendous metaphors which express His saving relationship toward the world. All appear in the book of John.*" These seven I AM statements were Jesus requesting His listeners to make some **PARADIGM SHIFTS**. One of these happened at the festival.

I AM – 2ⁿᵈ Time of 7

John 8:12 Then spake Jesus again unto them, saying, I am the light of the world: he that followeth me shall not walk in darkness, but shall have the light of life. (KJV)

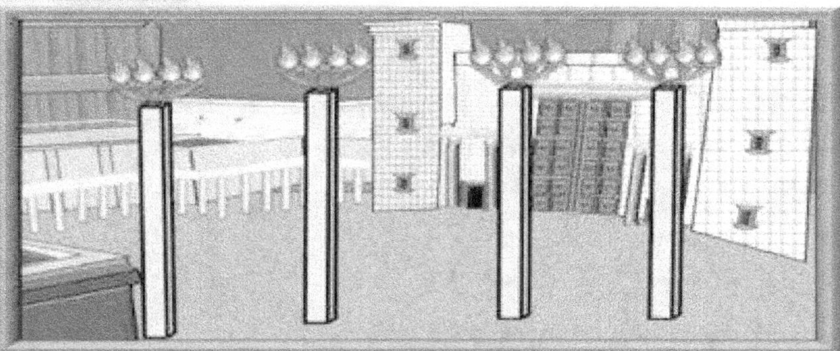

I AM – 3ʳᵈ Time of 7

John 10:7 Then said Jesus unto them again, Verily, verily, I say unto you, I am the door of the sheep.

John 10:8 All that ever came before me are thieves and robbers: but the sheep did not hear them. (KJV)

John 10:9 I am the door: by me if any man enter in, he shall be saved, and shall go in and out, and find pasture.

John 10:10 The thief cometh not, but for to steal, and to kill, and to destroy: I am come that they might have life, and that they might have it more abundantly. (KJV)

I AM – 4ᵗʰ Time of 7

John 10:11 I am the good shepherd: the good shepherd giveth his life for the sheep.

John 10:12 But he that is an hireling, and not the shepherd, whose own the sheep are not, seeth the wolf coming, and leaveth the sheep, and fleeth: and the wolf catcheth them, and scattereth the sheep. (KJV)

John 10:13 The hireling fleeth, because he is an hireling, and careth not for the sheep.

John 10:14 I am the good shepherd, and know my sheep, and am known of mine.

John 10:15 As the Father knoweth me, even so know I the Father: and I lay down my life for the sheep. (KJV)

I AM – 5ᵗʰ Time of 7

John 11:25 Jesus said unto her (i.e. Martha & Mary), I am the resurrection, and the life: he that believeth in me, though he were dead, yet shall he live:

John 11:26 And whosoever liveth and believeth in me shall never die. Believest thou this? (KJV)

John 11:43 And when he thus had spoken, he cried with a loud voice, Lazarus, come forth.

John 11:44 And he that was dead came forth, bound hand and foot with graveclothes: and his face was bound about with a napkin. Jesus saith unto them, Loose him, and let him go. (KJV)

I AM – 6th Time of 7

John 14:6 Jesus saith unto him, I am the way, the truth, and the life: no man cometh unto the Father, but by me.

John 14:7 If ye had known me, ye should have known my Father also: and from henceforth ye know him, and have seen him. (KJV)

John 14:12 Verily, verily, I say unto you, He that believeth on me, the works that I do shall he do also; and greater works than these shall he do; because I go unto my Father.

John 14:14 If ye shall ask any thing in my name, I will do it. (KJV)

I AM – 7th Time of 7

John 15:1 I am the true vine, and my Father is the husbandman.

John 15:2 Every branch in me that beareth not fruit he taketh away: and every branch that beareth fruit, he purgeth it, that it may bring forth more fruit. 3 Now ye are clean through the word which I have spoken unto you. (KJV)

John 15:4 Abide in me, and I in you. As the branch cannot bear fruit of itself, except it abide in the vine; no more can ye, except ye abide in me.

John 15:5 I am the vine, ye are the branches: He that abideth in me, and I in him, the same bringeth forth much fruit: for without me ye can do nothing. (KJV)

Final Thoughts

Why were the Pharisees so driven to wish to see Jesus annihilated? Jesus made several statements during this festival that made the Pharisees feel like their authority was being questioned and undermined. On more than one occasion, they had the impulse to stone Him; however, since the time of Jesus' death was scheduled for six months later, God created safe ways to help His Son escape their murderous plans. At one point, His followers formed a human chain to block the Pharisees' access to Him. After all, Jesus still had much groundwork to accomplish before He willingly sacrificed His life.

This was the Pharisees reaction when Jesus made this proclamation.

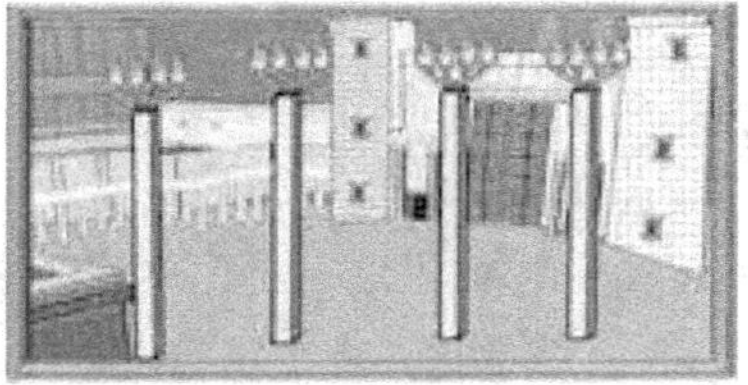

John 8:12 I am the light of the world: he that followeth me shall not walk in darkness, but shall have the light of life. (KJV)

FYI – This is a short synopsis of each statement made by the Pharisees and by Jesus.

"Your testimony is invalid because you have no witness." **John 8:13-18**	❶ "You may not know where I came from or where I am going; however, my testimony is valid." ❷ "Don't judge by human standards. I stand with the Father, who sent me here." ❸ "Your law requires two witnesses. My Father is one of my witnesses. My second witness is me. He authorizes me to speak His words on His behalf."
"Where is your Father?" **John 8:19-20**	❶ "You do not know me or my Father" ❷ "If you knew me, you would know my Father also."

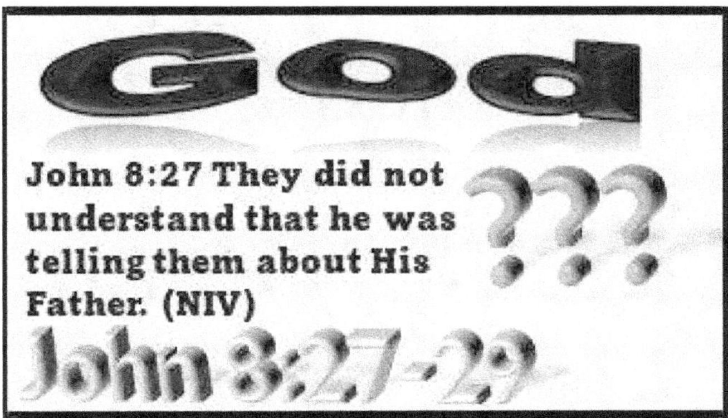

The Pharisees and some other Jews asked Jesus several more questions. Jesus gave many answers. To see more, please consider reading **John 8:31 to 58**. I will only list Jesus' rebuttals that likely angered them the most.

But first, let's back up a bit. You may recall that in **Genesis 12:1**, God instructed Abram, later to be renamed Abraham, to leave his father's house and go to a new land. Part of this was because his father and grandfather worshipped idols.

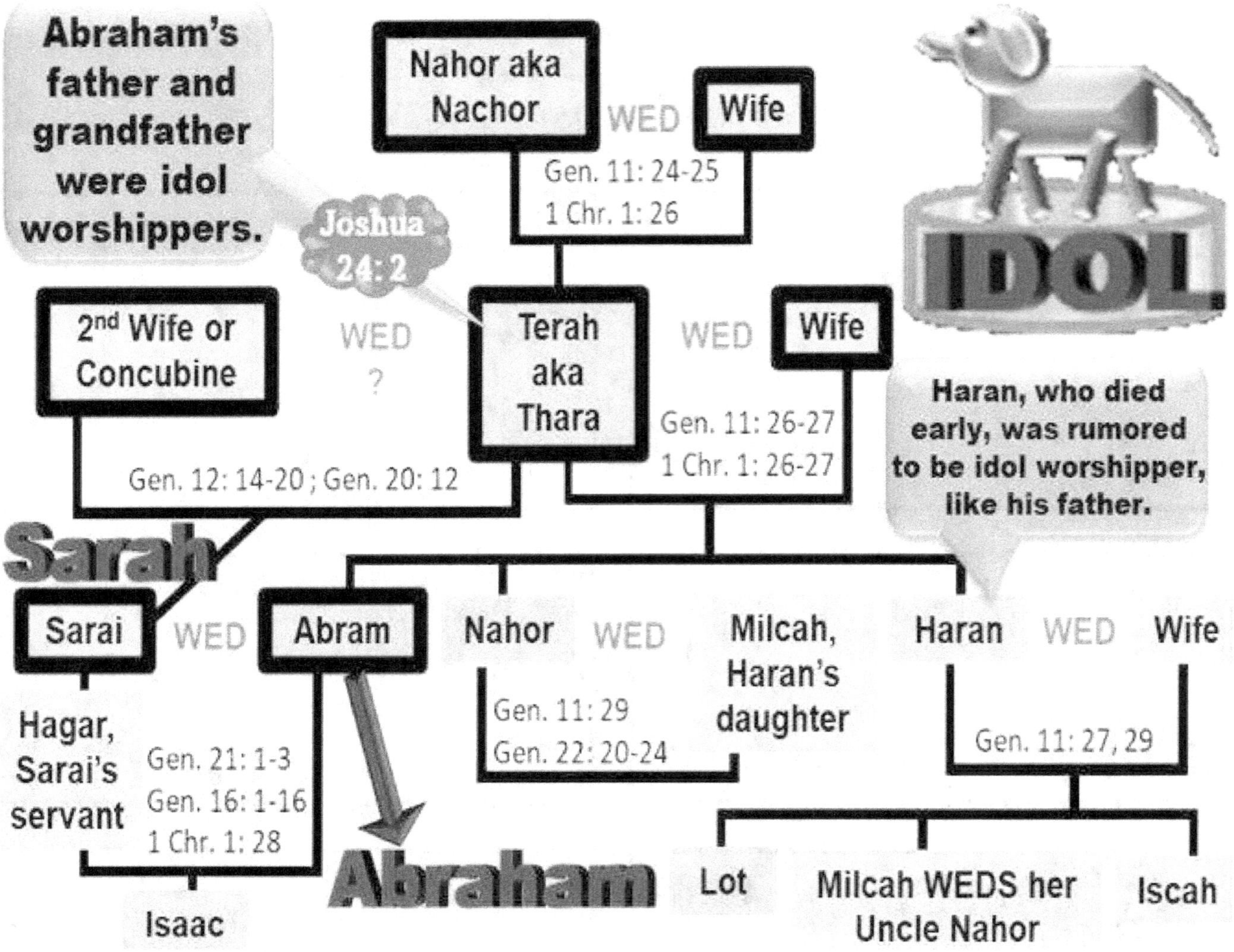

In exchange, God made the following promise.

Genesis 12:2 And I will make of thee a great nation, and I will bless thee, and make thy name great; and thou shalt be a blessing: 3 And I will bless them that bless thee, and curse him that curseth thee: and in thee shall all families of the earth be blessed. (KJV)

Fast forward roughly 500 years to the days of Moses. In Moses' 80th year, he led the Children of Israel from Egypt, the land of their former captivity, toward the Promised Land. During that forty-year journey, the Israelites turned to worshipping idols that included practices of indulging fleshly pleasures on repeat. So, God gave them the **10 Commandments**. (*Burning Bush incident found in Exodus 3.*)

The 10 Commandments

Exodus 20:3	1	You shall have no other God's before me.
Exodus 20:4-6	2	Thou shalt not make unto thee any graven images.
Exodus 20:7	3	Thou shalt not take the name of the Lord thy God in vain.
Exodus 20:8-11	4	Remember the Sabbath day and keep it Holy.
Exodus 20:12	5	Honor your father and mother.
Exodus 20:13	6	Thou shalt not kill.
Exodus 20:14	7	Thou shalt not commit adultery.
Exodus 20:15	8	Thou shalt not steal.
Exodus 20:16	9	Thou shall not bear false witness.
Exodus 20:17	10	You shall not covet.

Disclaimer: I apologize in advance to my Jewish brothers and sisters for giving this possibly over-simplified Gentile viewpoint.

Even so, there were times when the Israelites still turned to idols. So, it seemed God upped the ante and possibly gave as many as 613 mandates for the Children of Israel to observe, including the Ten Commandments. For a complete list embedded within Bible verses (with live links), see the Bibliography or Google the following title from Got Questions.org: '*What are the 613 commandments in the Old Testament Law?*'

With too much **idle time** on their hands, some of them turned to **idols**. By doing that, they broke the first and second commandments.

Fast forward another fifteen hundred years to about 30 AD. The Pharisees were so embroiled in observing those 613 mandates that they failed to see the bigger picture. Instead of fully worshipping God with a big G, they allegedly were making a god with a little g out of administering the mandates in their lives and the lives of the Jewish people. Jesus was attempting to rectify that situation.

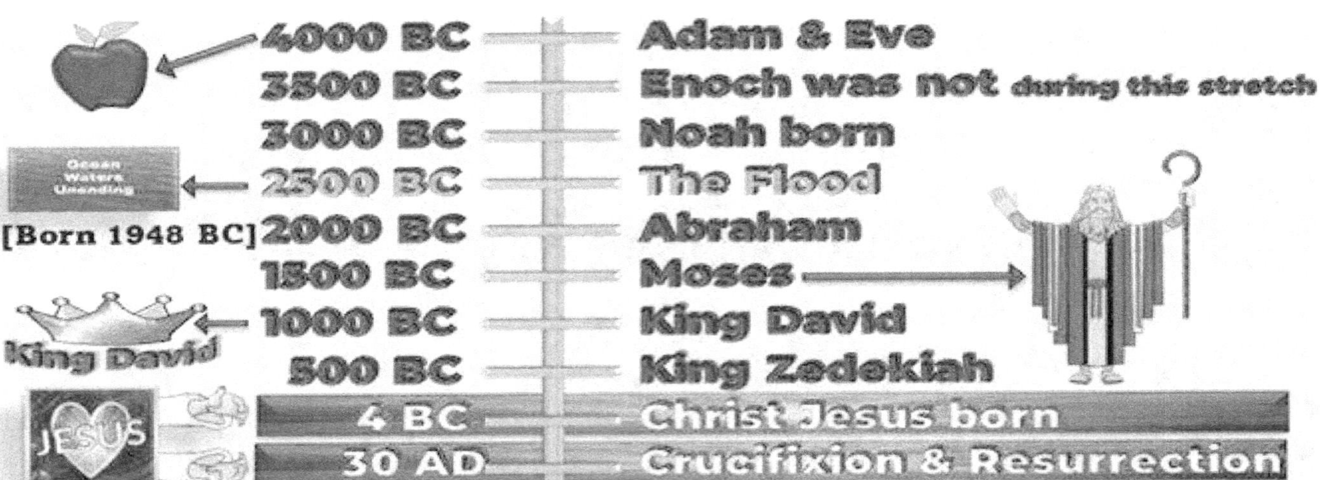

Here are six Bible verses describing the mindset the Pharisees displayed to Jesus during that festival.

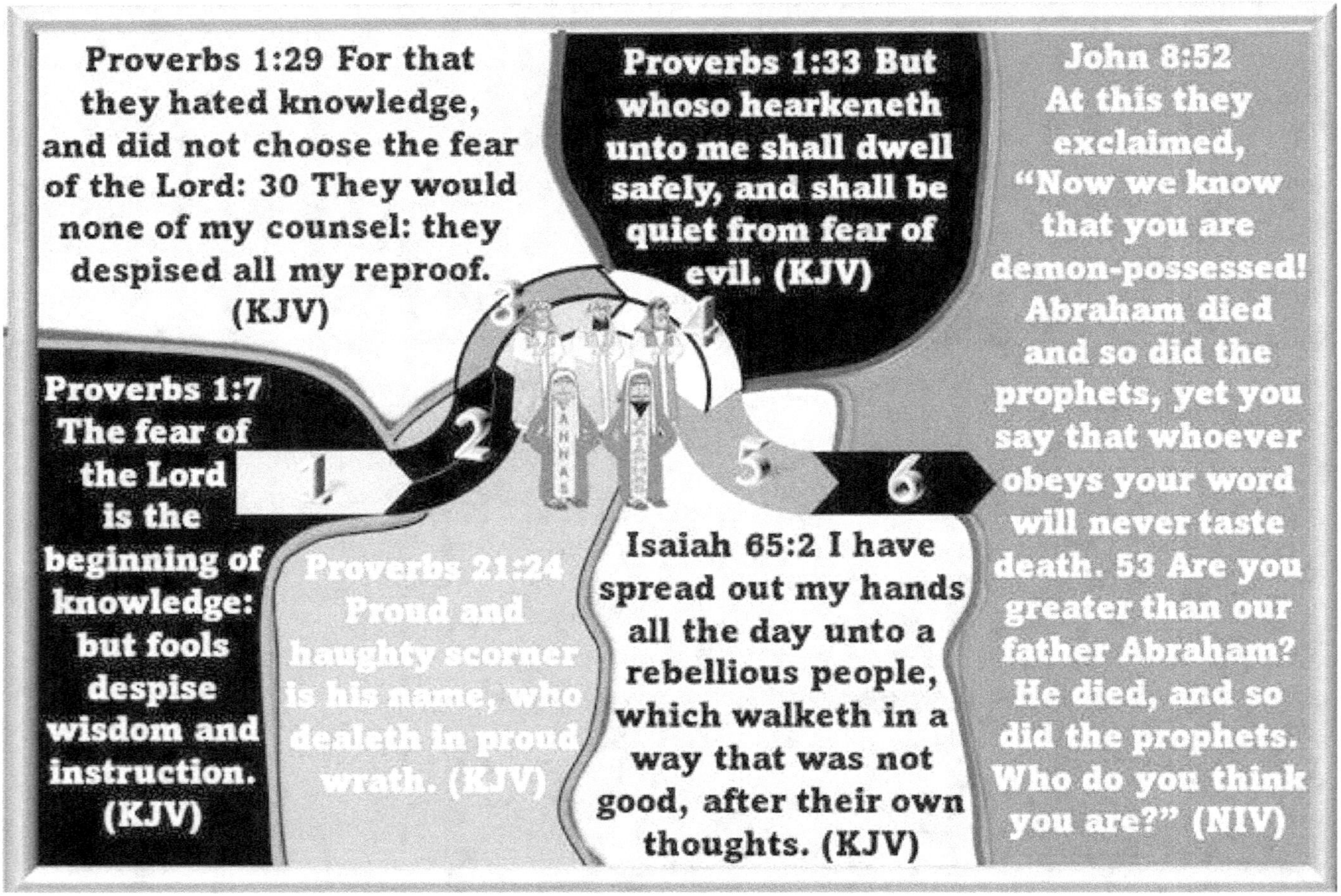

Proverbs 1:29 For that they hated knowledge, and did not choose the fear of the Lord: **30** They would none of my counsel: they despised all my reproof. (KJV)

Proverbs 1:33 But whoso hearkeneth unto me shall dwell safely, and shall be quiet from fear of evil. (KJV)

John 8:52 At this they exclaimed, "Now we know that you are demon-possessed! Abraham died and so did the prophets, yet you say that whoever obeys your word will never taste death. **53** Are you greater than our father Abraham? He died, and so did the prophets. Who do you think you are?" (NIV)

Proverbs 1:7 The fear of the Lord is the beginning of knowledge: but fools despise wisdom and instruction. (KJV)

Proverbs 21:24 Proud and haughty scorner is his name, who dealeth in proud wrath. (KJV)

Isaiah 65:2 I have spread out my hands all the day unto a rebellious people, which walketh in a way that was not good, after their own thoughts. (KJV)

Jesus tried to let them know, in **John 8:31-32**, "If you hold to my teaching, you are really my disciples. 32 Then you will know the truth, and the truth will set you free."

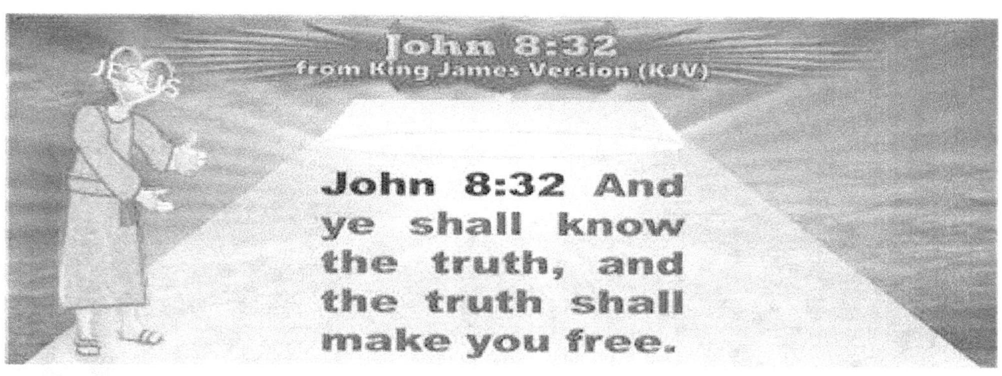

John 8:33 They answered him, "We are Abraham's descendants and have never been slaves of anyone. How can you say that we shall be set free?" (KJV)

That, of course, was an untrue statement. For decades and decades, the whole festival was dedicated to the fact that the Israelites were freed from being enslaved in Egypt. The Jewish people were also enslaved in Babylon. The Pharisees and Sanhedrin seemed determined to object to every word out of Jesus' mouth, regardless of its validity.

John 8:34 Jesus replied, "Very truly I tell you, everyone who sins is a slave to sin. 35 Now a slave has no permanent place in the family, but a son belongs to it forever. 36 So if the Son sets you free, you will be free indeed. 37 I know that you are Abraham's descendants. Yet you are looking for a way to kill me, because you have no room for my word. 38 I am telling you what I have seen in the Father's presence, and you are doing what you have heard from your father." (KJV)

These final two interactions between Jesus and the Pharisees sealed the deal. After that, they were more determined than ever to forego honoring the sixth and ninth commandments of not committing murder or bearing false witness. By fair means or foul, the Pharisees intended to eliminate Jesus.

FYI – This is a short synopsis of each statement made by the Pharisees and by Jesus.

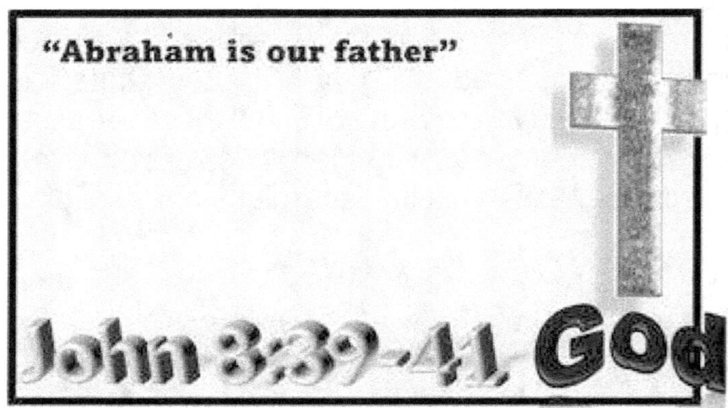

❶ "If you were Abraham's children, then you would do what Abraham did."

❷ "As it is, you are looking for a way to kill me, a man who has told you the truth that I heard from God. Abraham did not do such things."

❸ "You are doing the works of your own father."

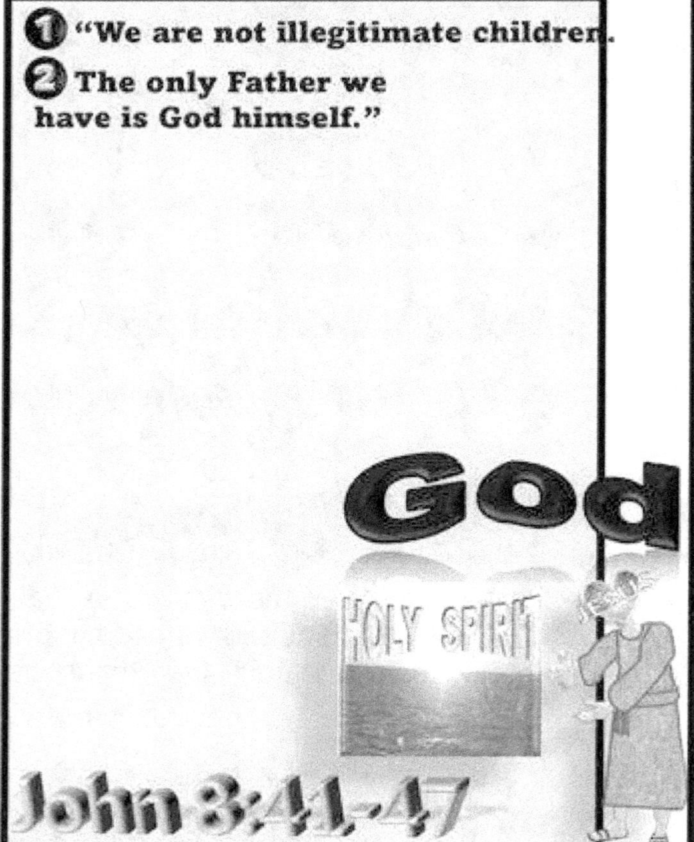

❶ "If God were your Father, you would love me, for I have come here from God. I have not come on my own; God sent me."

❷ "Why is my language not clear to you? Because you are unable to hear what I say."

❸ "You belong to your father, the devil, and you want to carry out your father's desires. He was a murderer from the beginning, not holding to the truth, for there is no truth in him. When he lies, he speaks his native language, for he is a liar and the father of lies."

❹ "Yet because I tell the truth, you do not believe me! Can any of you prove me guilty of sin? If I am telling the truth, why don't you believe me?"

❺ "Whoever belongs to God hears what God says. The reason you do not hear is that you do not belong to God."

What do you place your hope in?

YOUR WORDS AND ACTIONS CAST YOUR VOTE.

Is your hope in Christ? Then, your thoughts, words, and actions will likely demonstrate that fact.

Is your hope in fulfilling fleshly desires or accumulating wealth or other possessions? Then, your thoughts, words, and actions will likely demonstrate that fact, too.

You can become a member of Christ's family but must actively choose it. It is your free will choice to make.

It will not be authentic if you choose to follow Christ based on the fear that you might go to hell otherwise. You need to choose Christ because you authentically validate that by doing so, your life will be happier and so much better.

Sadly, there are some Christians who appear to be Christian by name only. Their thoughts, words, and actions draw people one or more steps away from Christ rather than closer to Christ. It is vital to be a good representative of this title. Being a compassionate and kind person is critical.

On the other hand, some people are a joy to be around as they are on fire for Christ. They shouldn't be too pushy or try to shove it down people's throats. They should let their lives model that their thoughts, words, and actions demonstrate Christ-like characteristics. In that way, people might be drawn to wanting to feel the same happiness and peace in their own lives.

Consider taking an internal inventory of your thoughts, words, and actions. Ask the **Holy Spirit** to alert you if any of your thoughts, words, or actions are not positively serving your life or the lives of the people around you. In other words, do not be spiritually blind. Take the blinders off and examine what you do or have done.

If necessary, ask forgiveness of Almighty God. With the help of Jesus and the Holy Spirit, come up with a new plan for a way of thinking, talking, and doing.

After all, God created us in His image and likeness -- not the other way around. We need to be aware that at all times, there are **RECORDING ANGELS** registering whether our thoughts, words, and actions comply with God's will. We also should be vigilant and aware that Satan is going to do his level best to trip us up. Upon request, the Holy Spirit will put safeguards in place.

1. What happened during the first trial between Jesus and the former High Priest, Annas?

2. Why did one of the officers serving Annas slap Jesus? What do you think will happen to Him on Judgment Day?

3. What happened during the second trial between Jesus and the current High Priest, Caiaphas?

4. You will recall that after the cock crowed, Jesus turned to look at Peter. If you were Peter, what would you be feeling after that happened? Why?

5. What happened during the third trial when Jesus met with the Sanhedrin around sunrise on that Friday?

6. To what level does knowing about what Jesus suffered for our sakes inspire you to want to love and follow Jesus even more closely? Describe how these details about Him make you think and feel?

7. Why did the Jewish elders in Bible days and even people today have such a hard time accepting what it states in John 14:6 that Jesus is "the way and truth and the life, and no one comes to the Father except through" Him? Do you agree or disagree with these words of Jesus? Please explain.

8. Describe what happens during the 8-day Feast of Tabernacles.

9. Why do you think it is important for you to let your light shine before humankind? [Matthew 5:14-16]

10. In John 9:39, Jesus described spiritual blindness as He said, "For judgment I have come into this world, so that the blind will see and those who see will become blind." In what ways were the Pharisees spiritually blind? Do you feel like you are spiritually blind in any way? If so, in what ways can you fix this?

11. Describe the seven "I AM" statements made by Jesus.

12. Analyze in what ways your words and actions either draw people closer to Christ or further away from Christ. Journal about this or discuss.

OUT OF GUILT, JUDAS TRIES TO RETURN MONEY TO PRIESTS

Judas Iscariot was a lukewarm Christian. He might have been on fire when he first began following Jesus three years prior, but those days were long over. Judas could fool his fellow Disciples into believing him to be devout, but Jesus was well aware of his waning affections.

Disciple John spent his final years exiled on the Greek island called Patmos in the Aegean Sea. During that time, he wrote the book of Revelations. He might have been reminded of Judas Iscariot when he wrote the following verses.

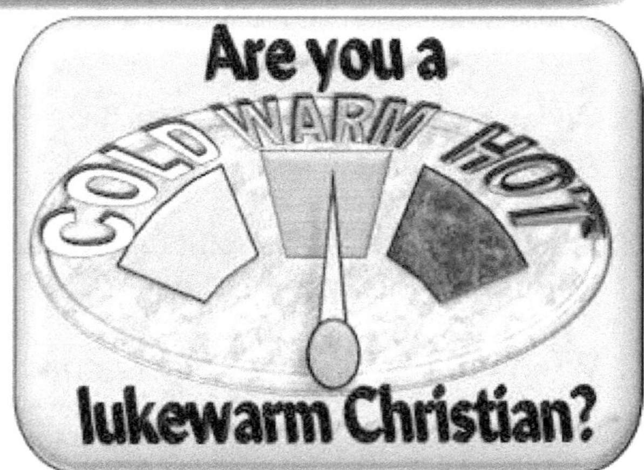

Revelation 3:14 "To the angel of the church in Laodicea write: These are the words of the Amen, the faithful and true witness, the ruler of God's creation.

Revelation 3:15 I know your deeds, that you are neither cold nor hot. I wish you were either one or the other!

Revelation 3:16 So, because you are lukewarm—neither hot nor cold—I am about to spit you out of my mouth. (NIV)

Sadly, Judas Iscariot burnt all his bridges. He betrayed Jesus in such a manner that he killed the trust of his friends and was destined for hell after he died. He felt horrible guilt; however, it might have been guilt or regret for being caught rather than genuine repentance. God will not tolerate lukewarm apologies or lukewarm Christians.

Matthew 27:3 When Judas, who had betrayed him, saw that Jesus was condemned, he was seized with remorse and returned the thirty pieces of silver to the chief priests and the elders.

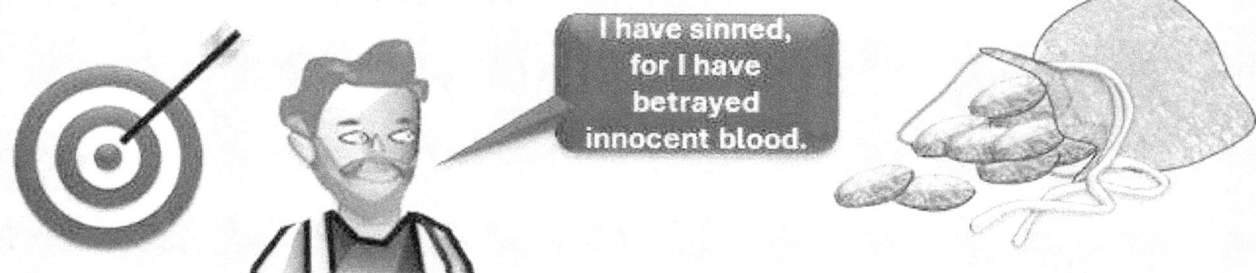

Matthew 27:4 "I have sinned," he said, "for I have betrayed innocent blood." "What is that to us?" they replied. "That's your responsibility."

Matthew 27:5 So Judas threw the money into the temple and left. Then he went away and hanged himself.

Matthew 27:6 The chief priests picked up the coins and said, "It is against the law to put this into the treasury, since it is blood money."

Matthew 27:7 So they decided to use the money to buy the potter's field as a burial place for foreigners.

Matthew 27:8 That is why it has been called the Field of Blood to this day.

Matthew 27:9 Then what was spoken by Jeremiah the prophet was fulfilled: "They took the thirty pieces of silver, the price set on him by the people of Israel, 10 and they used them to buy the potter's field, as the Lord commanded me." (NIV)

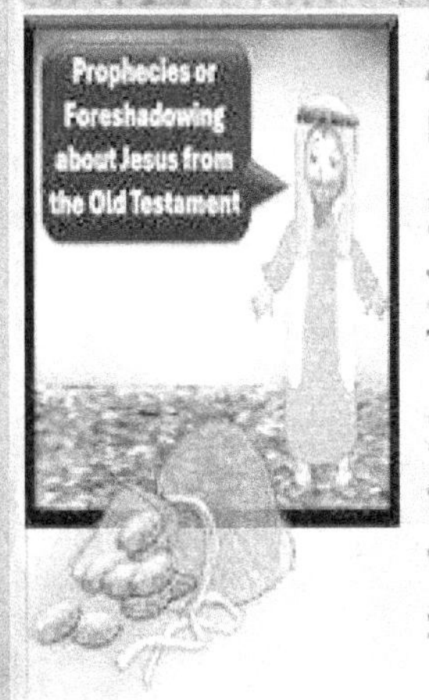

Zechariah (NIV) was written by the Prophet Zechariah. He also had an experience with thirty pieces of silver.

Zechariah 11:12 Then I said to them, "If it seems good to you, give me my wages; but if not, keep them." And they weighed out as my wages thirty pieces of silver.

Zechariah 11:13 Then the LORD said to me, "Throw it to the potter"—the lordly price at which I was priced by them. So, I took the thirty pieces of silver and threw them into the house of the LORD, to the potter.

FYI – "The lordly price" was meant sarcastically.

During the Last Supper

Matthew 26:24 The Son of Man will go just as it is written about him. But woe to that man who betrays the Son of Man! It would be better for him if he had not been born. (NIV)

During prayers in the Garden of Gethsemane

John 17:12 While I was with them, I protected them and kept them safe by that name you gave me. None has been lost except the one doomed to destruction so that Scripture would be fulfilled. (NIV)

Consequences for lukewarm Christians and people denying Christ.

Hebrews 10:26 If we deliberately keep on sinning after we have received the knowledge of the truth, no sacrifice for sins is left, 27 but only a fearful expectation of judgment and of raging fire that will consume the enemies of God.

Hebrews 10:28 Anyone who rejected the law of Moses died without mercy on the testimony of two or three witnesses.

Hebrews 10:29 How much more severely do you think someone deserves to be punished who has trampled the Son of God underfoot, who has treated as an unholy thing the blood of the covenant that sanctified them, and who has insulted the Spirit of grace?

Hebrews 10:30 For we know him who said, "It is mine to avenge; I will repay," and again, "The Lord will judge his people."

Hebrews 10:31 It is a dreadful thing to fall into the hands of the living God. (NIV)

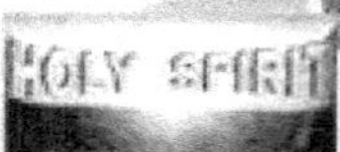

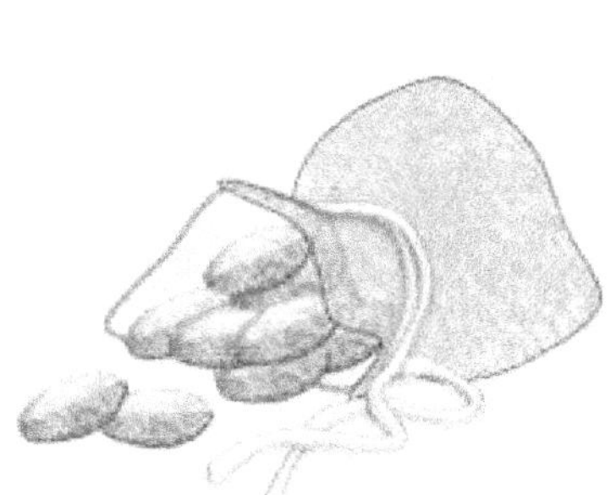

1. What does it mean to be a lukewarm Christian? Why does God prefer you to be either hot or cold rather than lukewarm?

2. In what ways did Judas demonstrate that he was a lukewarm Christian?

3. If Judas had truly repented for betraying Jesus and for stealing funds from the money bags he carried on behalf of Jesus and the Disciples, do you think he could have been sent to Heaven after he died?

4. Why was it wrong for Judas to commit suicide instead of trying to right the wrongs that he did? What do you think he should have done instead?

5. Share the story of how Saul of Tarsus converted to Christianity and became known as Paul instead. What crimes was he guilty of committing before he was blinded on the road to Damascus? See Acts 8:1-3 and Acts 9:1-19.

6. What did Paul have to do to become forgiven?

7. Do you think the other Disciples found it easy or hard to forgive Paul? How long do you think it took to convince them that he was sincere in his repentance?

8. Describe the wonderful contributions Paul made to the Bible and Christianity.

9. Share your thoughts about when you have found it challenging to forgive others. Why is it vital that we endeavor to forgive others?

10. What has Jesus commanded us to do regarding forgiveness?

4TH OF 6 TRIALS FOR JESUS

The Sanhedrin elders and soldiers took the bound Jesus to Pilate.

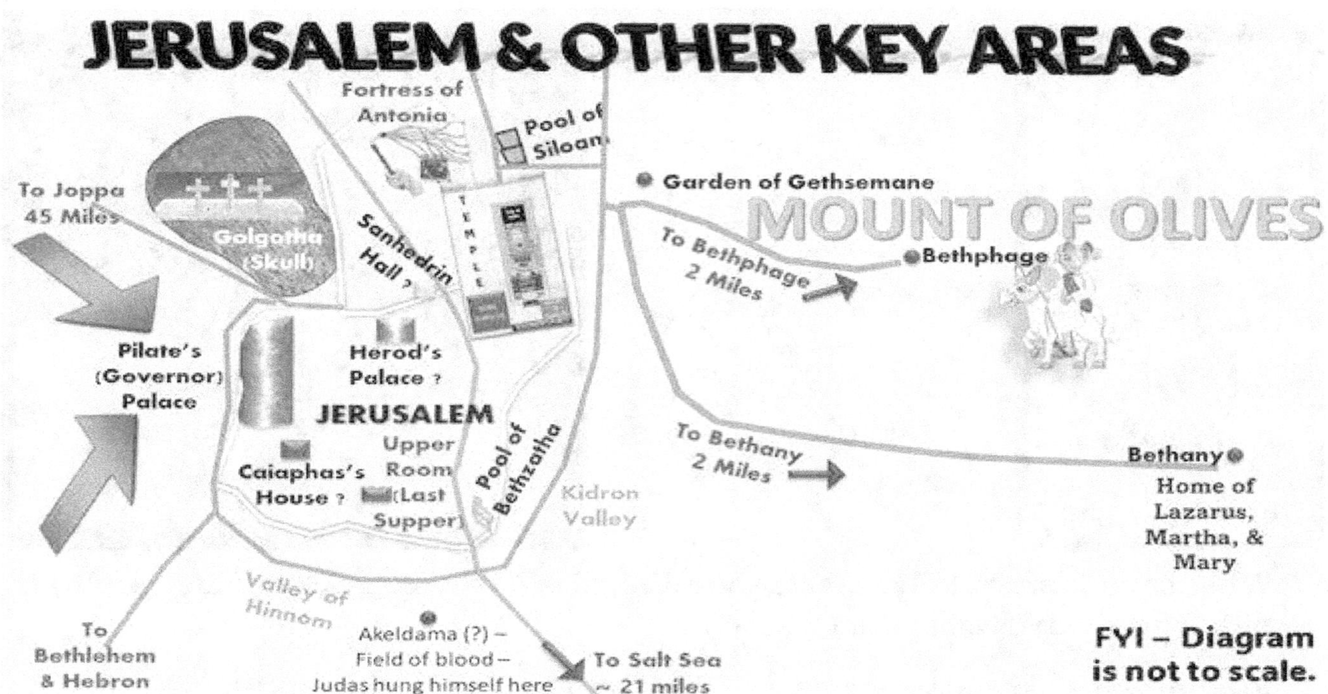

4th Trial for Jesus – 1st time with Pilate

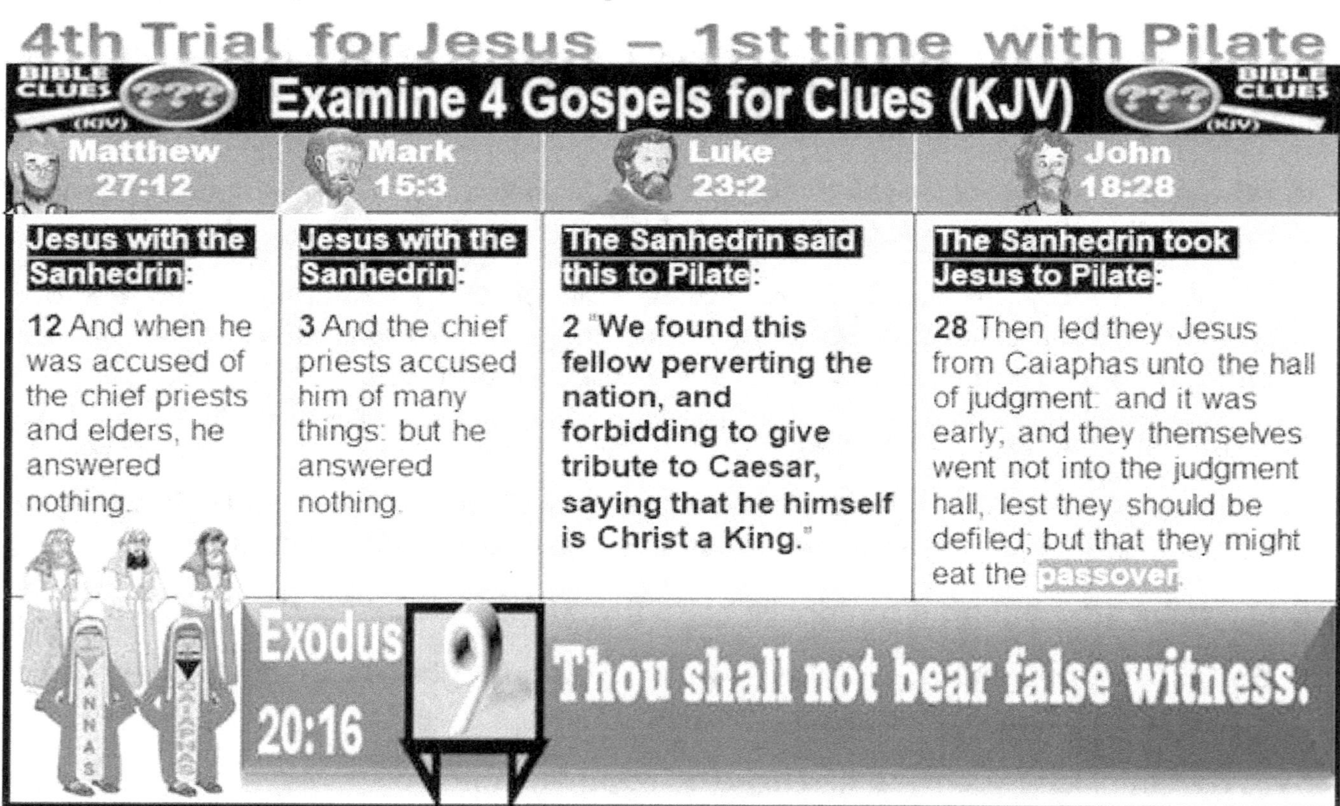

Matthew 27:12	Mark 15:3	Luke 23:2	John 18:28
Jesus with the Sanhedrin:	**Jesus with the Sanhedrin:**	**The Sanhedrin said this to Pilate:**	**The Sanhedrin took Jesus to Pilate:**
12 And when he was accused of the chief priests and elders, he answered nothing.	**3** And the chief priests accused him of many things: but he answered nothing.	**2** "We found this fellow perverting the nation, and forbidding to give tribute to Caesar, saying that he himself is Christ a King."	**28** Then led they Jesus from Caiaphas unto the hall of judgment: and it was early; and they themselves went not into the judgment hall, lest they should be defiled; but that they might eat the passover.

4th Trial for Jesus – 1st time with Pilate

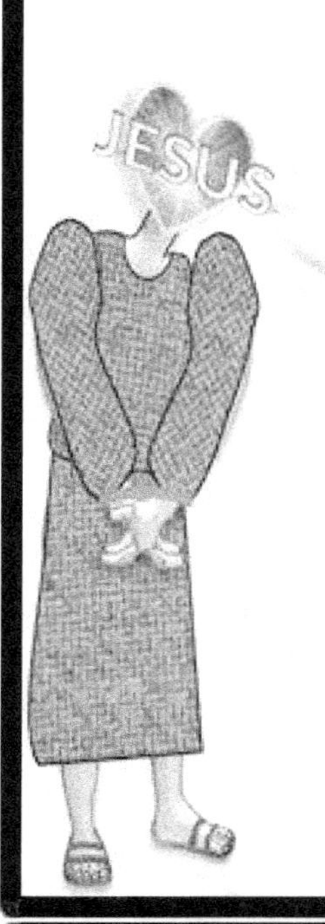

John 18:35 Pilate answered, Am I a Jew? Thine own nation and the chief priests have delivered thee unto me: what hast thou done?
John 18:36 Jesus answered, My kingdom is not of this world: if my kingdom were of this world, then would my servants fight, that I should not be delivered to the Jews: but now is my kingdom not from hence.

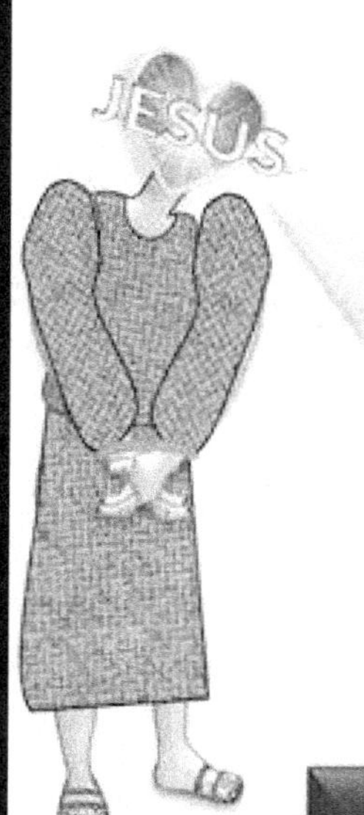

John 18:37 Pilate therefore said unto him, Art thou a king then?
John 18:37 Jesus answered, Thou sayest that I am a king. To this end was I born, and for this cause came I into the world, that I should bear witness unto the truth. Every one that is of the truth heareth my voice.
John 18:38 Pilate saith unto him, What is truth? And when he had said this, he went out again unto the Jews, and saith unto them, I find in him no fault at all.

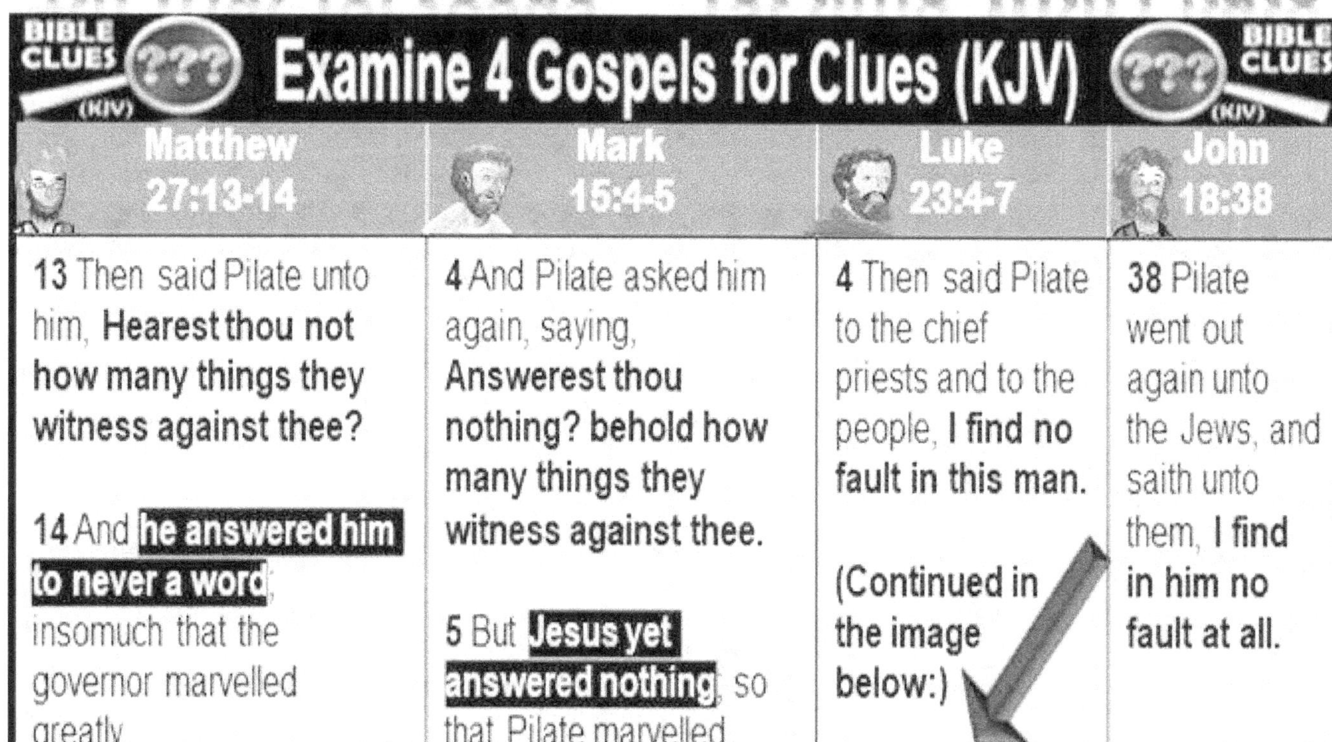

Examine 4 Gospels for Clues (KJV)

Matthew 27:13-14	Mark 15:4-5	Luke 23:4-7	John 18:38
13 Then said Pilate unto him, **Hearest thou not how many things they witness against thee?** 14 And **he answered him to never a word**; insomuch that the governor marvelled greatly.	4 And Pilate asked him again, saying, **Answerest thou nothing? behold how many things they witness against thee.** 5 But **Jesus yet answered nothing**, so that Pilate marvelled.	4 Then said Pilate to the chief priests and to the people, **I find no fault in this man.** (Continued in the image below:)	38 Pilate went out again unto the Jews, and saith unto them, **I find in him no fault at all.**

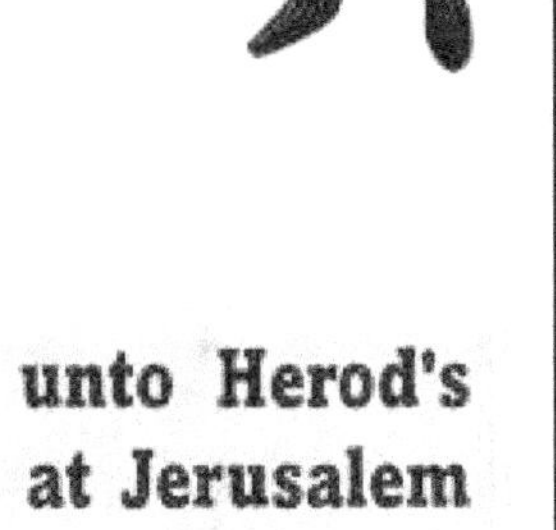

Luke 23:7 And as soon as he knew that he belonged unto Herod's jurisdiction, he sent him to Herod, who himself also was at Jerusalem at that time.

THE WIFE OF PONTIUS PILATE HAD A DREAM ABOUT JESUS

At conclusion of 4th Trial for Jesus

Examine 4 Gospels for Clues (KJV)

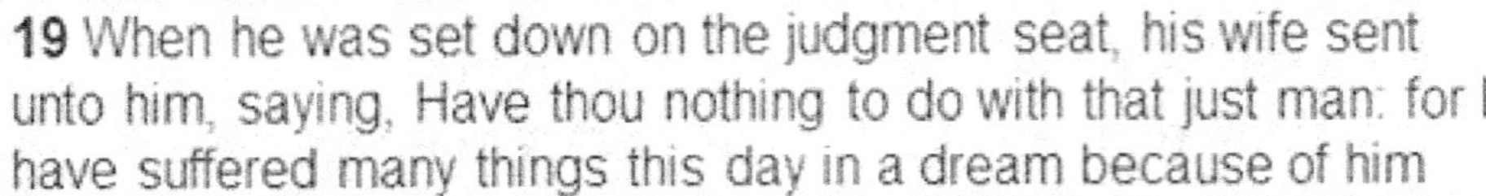

Matthew 27:19	Mark, Luke, & John
19 When he was set down on the judgment seat, his wife sent unto him, saying, Have thou nothing to do with that just man: for I have suffered many things this day in a dream because of him	No Reference to this Topic.

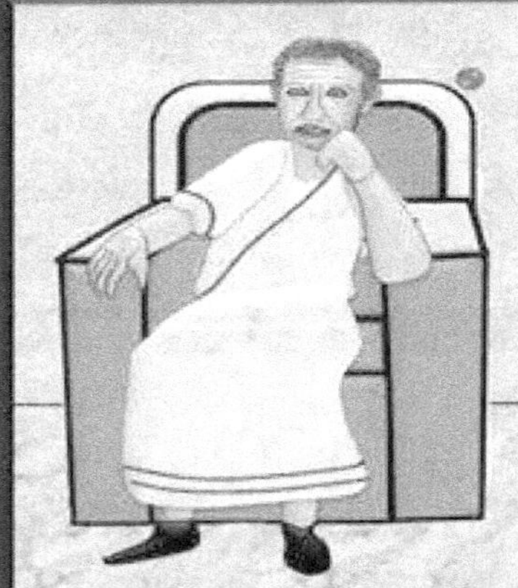

Google quote

What did the Romans believe about dreams in the first century?

"In Ancient Greece and Rome, the predominant view of dreams was that they were divine in origin. This view was held not only in theory but also in practice with the establishment of various dream-oracles and dream interpretation manuals Oneirocritica was the name of those manuals."

5TH OF 6 TRIALS FOR JESUS

The Sanhedrin elders and soldiers were forced to take Jesus to Herod.

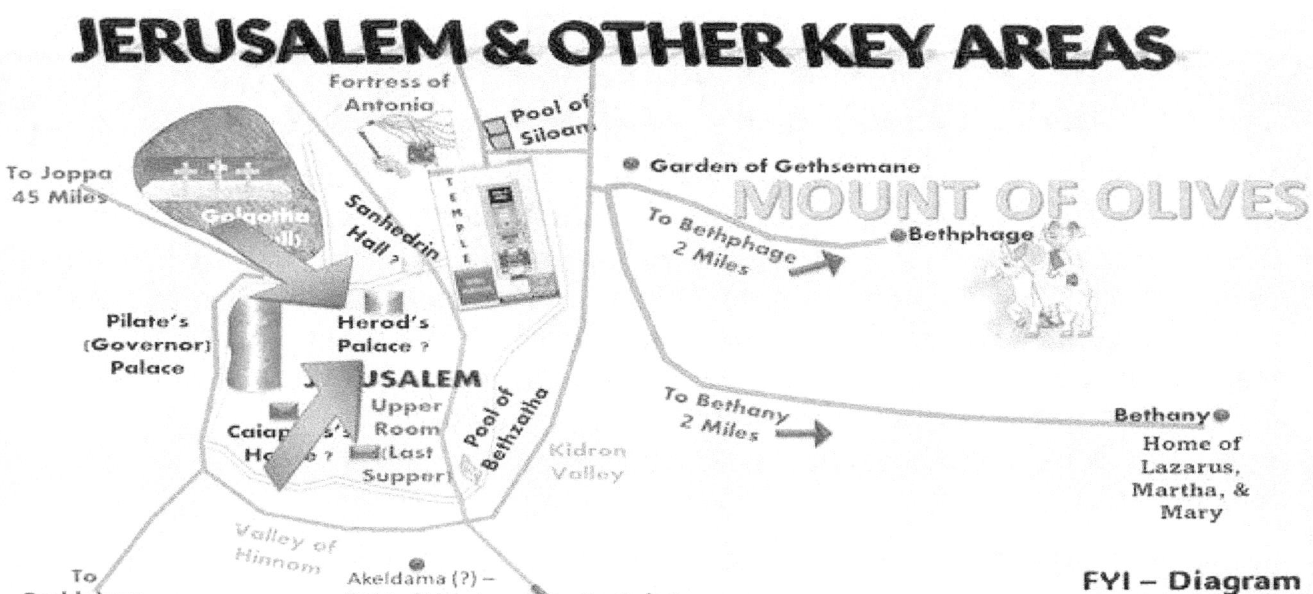

5th Trial for Jesus – Time with Herod

BIBLE CLUES (KJV) ??? Examine 4 Gospels for Clues (KJV) ??? BIBLE CLUES (KJV)	
Matthew, Mark, & John	**Luke 23:8-12**
No Reference to this Topic.	8 And when Herod saw Jesus, he was exceeding glad: for he was desirous to see him of a long season, because he had heard many things of him; and he hoped to have seen some miracle done by him.
	9 Then he questioned with him in many words; but he answered him nothing.
	10 And the chief priests and scribes stood and vehemently accused him.
	11 And Herod with his men of war set him at nought, and mocked him, and arrayed him in a gorgeous robe, and sent him again to Pilate.
	12 And the same day Pilate and Herod were made friends together: for before they were at enmity between themselves.

6TH OF 6 TRIALS FOR JESUS

The Sanhedrin elders and soldiers determinedly returned Jesus to Pilate.

6th Trial for Jesus – 2nd time with Pilate

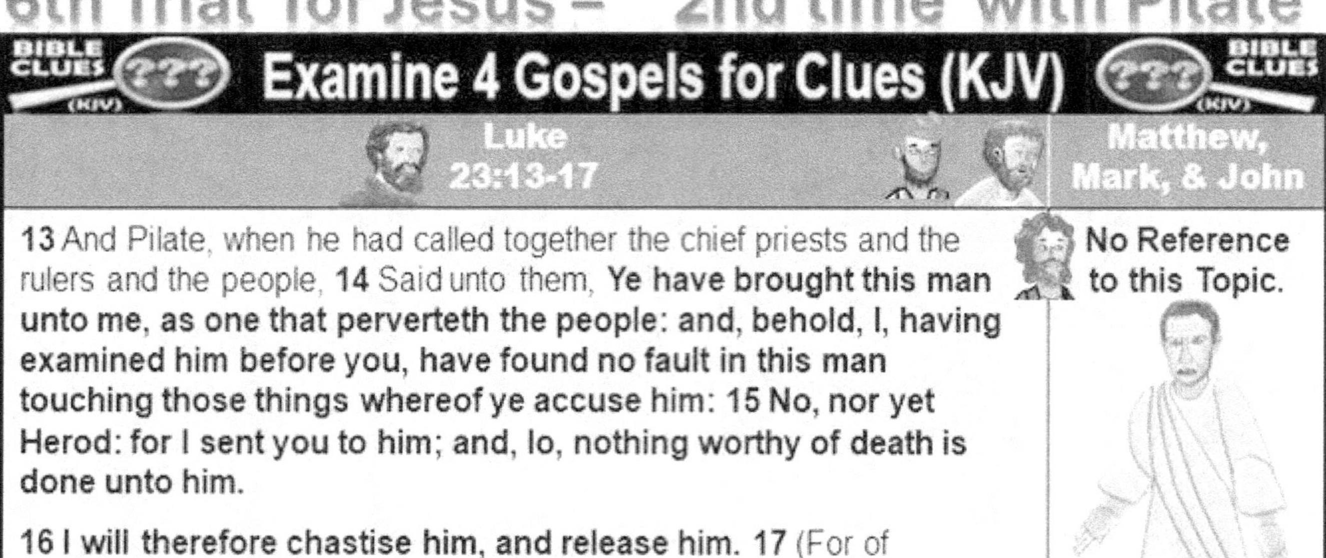

At the Passover Seder each year, the Roman governor would release one prisoner in Jerusalem. At this time, Pontius Pilate was the governor. It was his duty to present two potential prisoners to the Jewish people. It would be their prerogative to choose one of those two prisoners to be set free.

We learn about this by reading **Matthew 27:15-18, Matthew 27:20-26, Mark 15:6-15, Luke 23:18-25, John 18:39-40**, and **John 19:1**.

This year, option one was Barabbas. He was currently serving a prison sentence for a murder he committed during an insurrection or sedition made in the city. He was also guilty of theft. The second option was Jesus. Pilate was convinced Jesus was innocent and undeserving of death.

Matthew 27:18 and **Mark 15:10** stated that Pilate was aware that **ENVY** was the motivator behind the Pharisees' desire to see Jesus killed.

Pilate couldn't avoid hearing the rumble of voices, as stated in **Luke 23:21**, calling for him to crucify Jesus.

Pilate was willing to try to appease the Jews by offering to chastise (i.e., scourge) Jesus before releasing Him. In **Luke 23:22**, Pilate said, **"Why, what evil hath he done? I have found no cause of death in him: I will therefore chastise him, and let him go."**

But the people, egged on by the Sanhedrin (and perhaps bribed or threatened), would have no part of this.

In **Matthew 27:17**, Pilate asked the crowd:

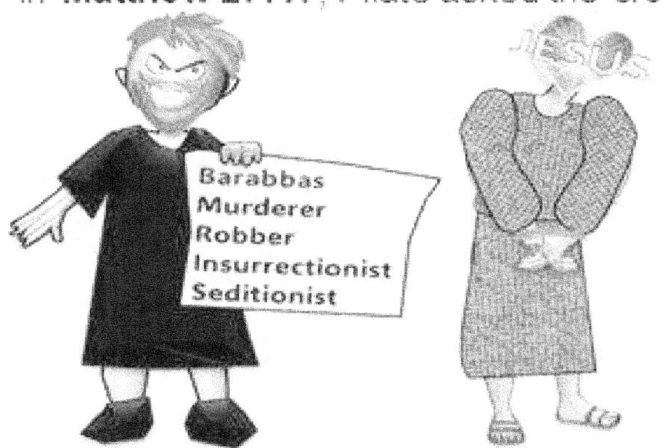

Pilate heard the crowd demand, in **Luke 23:18**, "Away with this man, and release unto us Barabbas." We learn that the people responded similarly in **John 18:40**, "Not this man, but Barabbas."

The rumble of voices to crucify Jesus was getting louder and more frequent.

Pilate released Barabbas unto them.

During this sixth and final trial, four significant and tragic things happened:

1 The crowd chose to have the murderer, Barabbas, released instead of Jesus.

2 Even though Pilate believed Jesus was an innocent man, he allowed his Roman soldiers to scourge/whip Jesus 39 to 40 times.

3 The Roman soldiers overheard Pilate referring to Jesus as the King of the Jews. The soldiers, therefore, decided to make sport of Jesus in a most cruel manner that included pressing a Crown of Thorns into Jesus' scalp.

4 Pilate gave the Sanhedrin and the crowd one last chance to recant their demand to crucify Jesus. Yet, even though they saw he had most of the skin ripped from his backside, was bleeding heavily, and even had blood dripping from under the Crown of Thorns, no one appeared to demonstrate any mercy. They still demanded that the Romans should crucify Jesus.

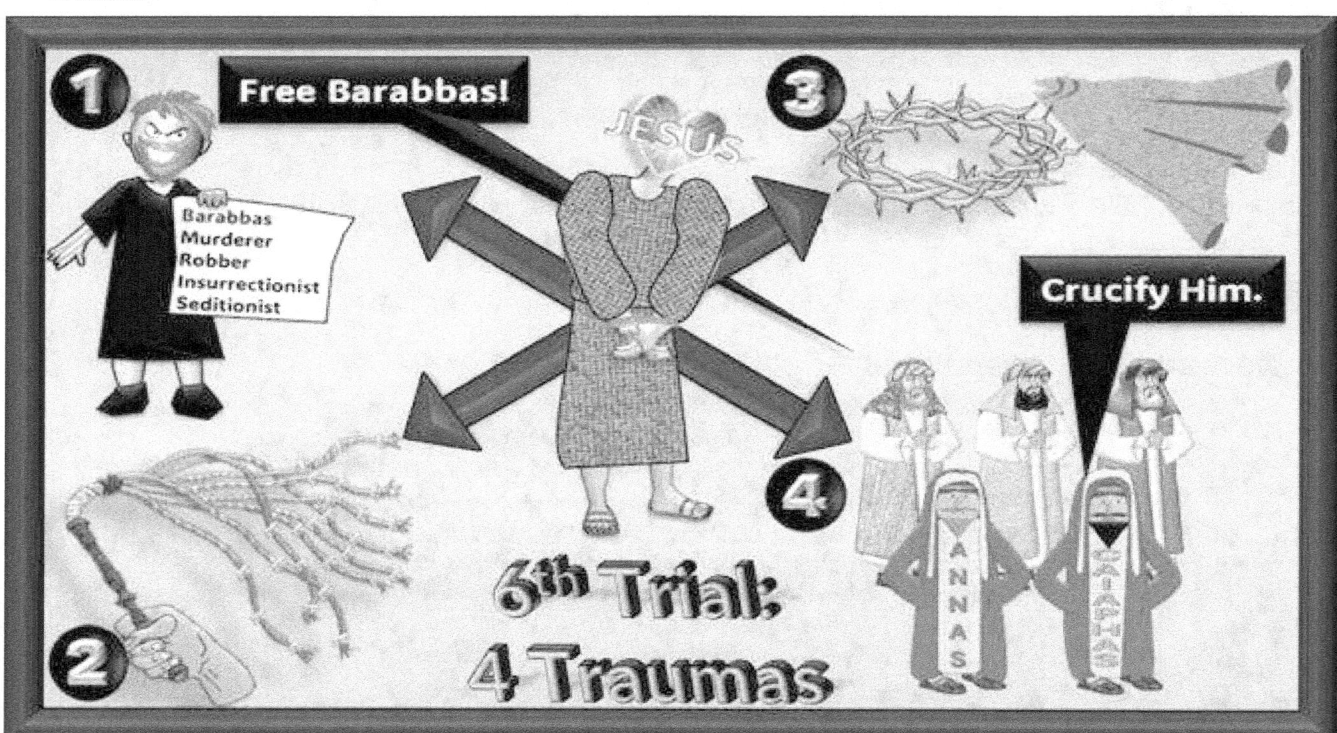

Pilate washed his hands.

That is when Pilate washed his hands to represent that he did not want anybody to convict him for shedding the blood of an innocent man. The crowd, egged on by the Sanhedrin, blithely responded, "His blood be on us and our children."

We can read about the Scourging and the Crown of Thorns torture in **Matthew 27:26-31**, **Mark 15:15-20**, and **John 19:1-5**. The book of Luke, in **Luke 23:16**, only mentions the scourging.

So, Jesus must have been temporarily dismissed by Pilate so that his soldiers could lead Him away to be scourged. The King James Version of the Books of Matthew, Mark, and John used the term '*scourging*,' whereas, the Book of Luke used 'chastise.'

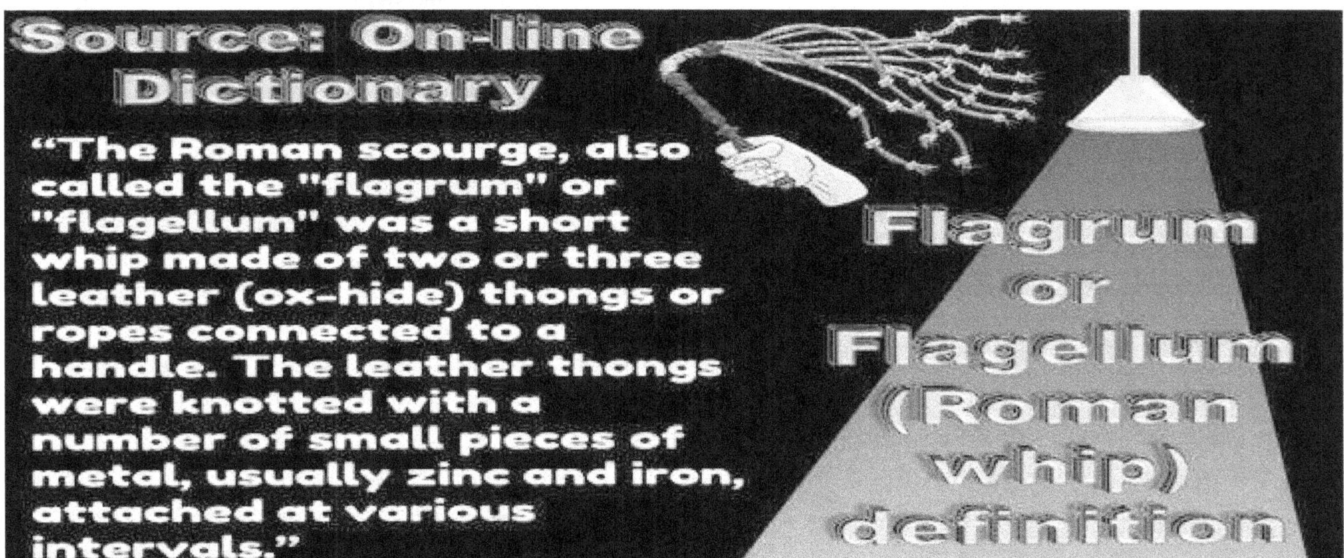

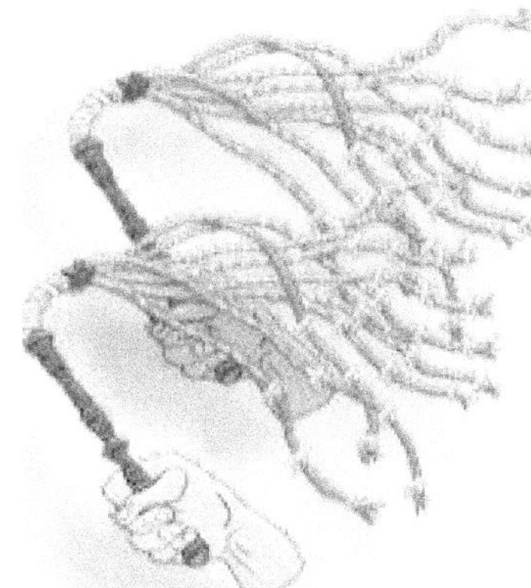

The Bible does not mention how many times Jesus was whipped. According to historians from that period, when a prisoner was scheduled for crucifixion, the Roman soldiers would scourge them 39 to 40 times in advance. After all, they didn't want the prisoner to die too soon. They wanted it to be a slow, lingering death.

FYI - Other Bible references to scourging can be found in **Deuteronomy 25:1-3** and **2 Corinthians 11:24**. The first one involves Moses receiving directions from the Lord regarding the Israelites. In the second, Paul stated, "Of the Jews five times received I forty stripes save one."

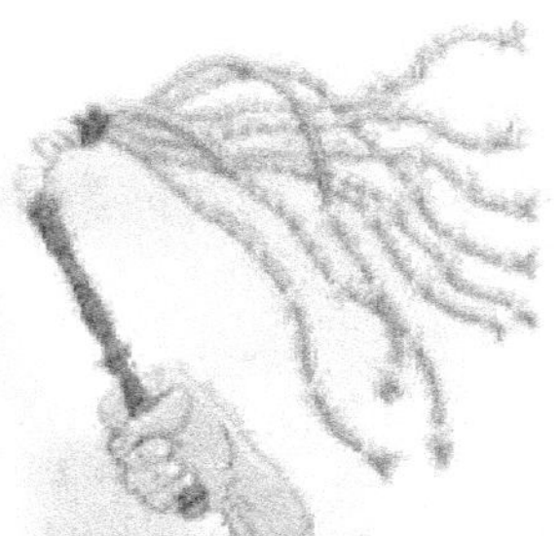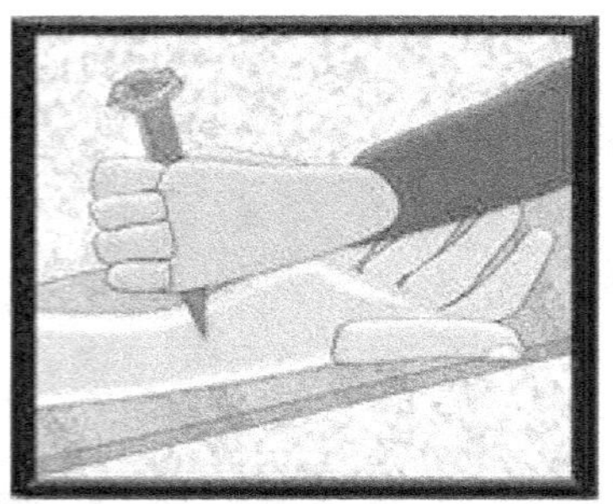

> Isaiah 53:5 But he was wounded for our transgressions, he was bruised for our iniquities: the chastisement of our peace was upon him; and with his stripes we are healed. 6 All we like sheep have gone astray; we have turned every one to his own way; and the LORD hath laid on him the iniquity of us all. (KJV)

I cannot fully describe how much those quotes convicted me. It was as if Jesus was saying, "You realize that when those two Roman soldiers whipped me 40 (or 39) times, I took each whip lash for you." Then, I can picture Him pointing to each of us as He repeated, with each crack of the whip, "You are worth it!"

When the Roman soldiers hammered the nails into His wrists and His ankles, He nodded His loving head in our direction as if to say, "I took that nail for you. I was determined to pay your ransom in full so that you may be forever free of Satan's hold. Do you know why? Because you are my beloved child whom I dearly love!"

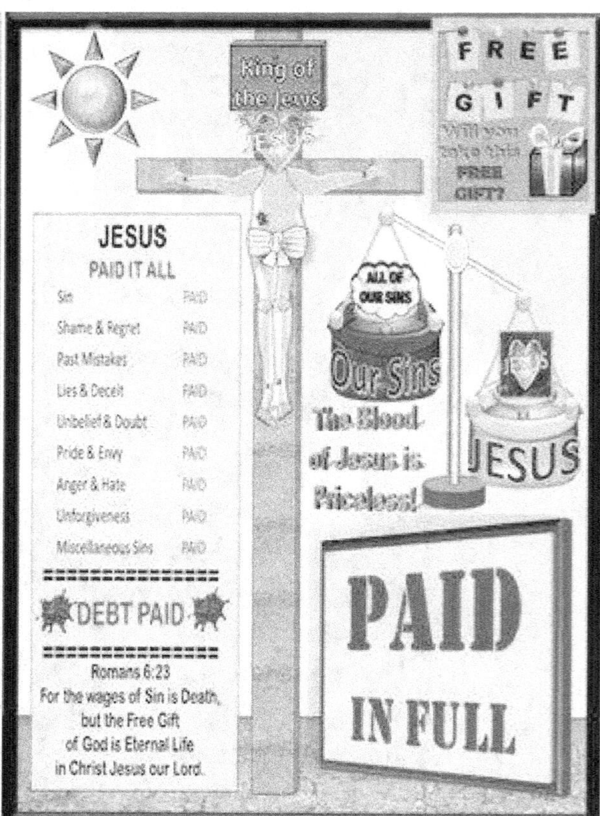

JERUSALEM & OTHER KEY AREAS

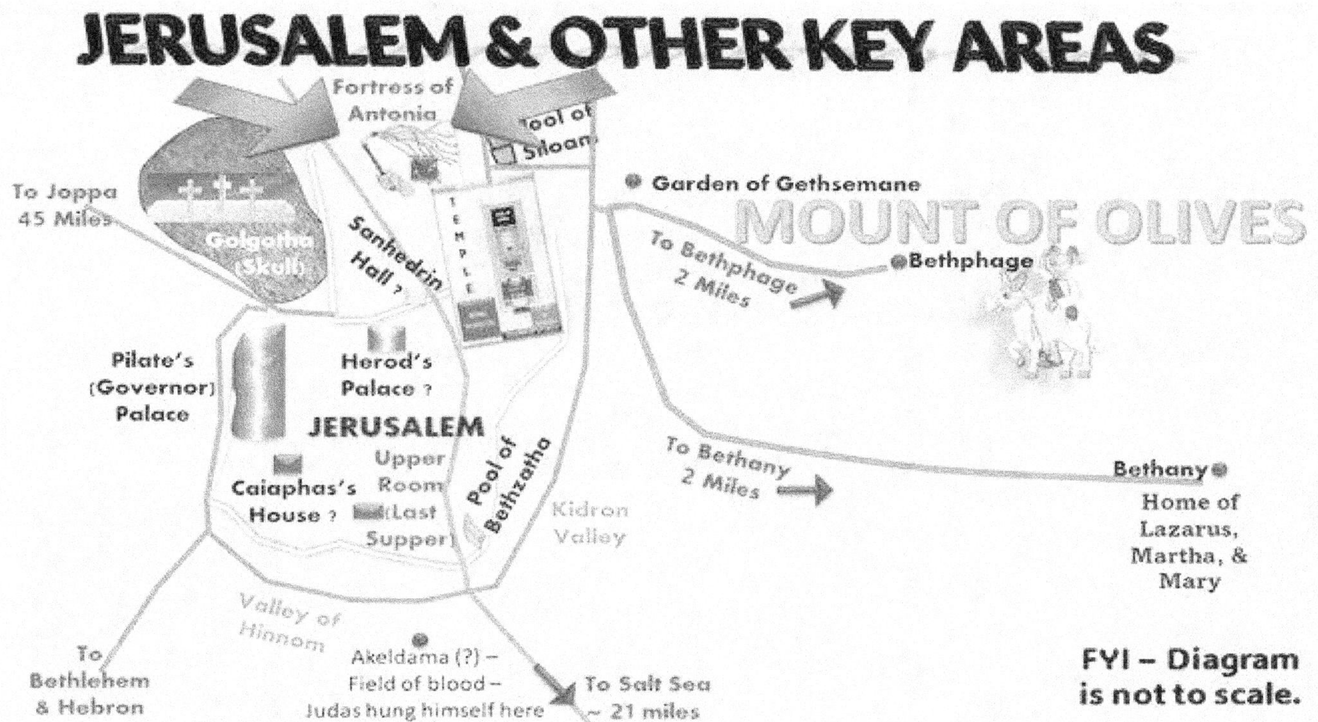

After the scourging, a whole band of soldiers led Jesus into the common hall that was called the Praetorium. It is unclear how many soldiers took part in this practice. They had overheard Pilate calling Him the King of the Jews. So, in revenge, they decided to try to heap humiliation on Jesus' head - literally and figuratively.

They stripped Jesus. Matthew states that they put a scarlet robe on him. Mark and John noted that the robe was purple. Since John witnessed the crucifixion, it is possible he also witnessed what color robe they placed upon Jesus.

> FYI – Do you recall how painful it is to rip off a band aid – especially if you have hair on your skin? Multiply that by 1000 for the pain of ripping off one bloody outfit and replacing it with another.

Sadly, since we know that the soldiers were smoting Jesus on His head, that would indicate that the thorns were being pounded deeper into His skull as a result. *Sigh!*

Mark 15:19 also states they were "bowing their knees worshipped him."

Matthew 27:31 and **Mark 15:20** describe that the soldiers removed the robe and put him back in His clothes.

John described it a little differently. See what he stated in **John 19:4-5**.

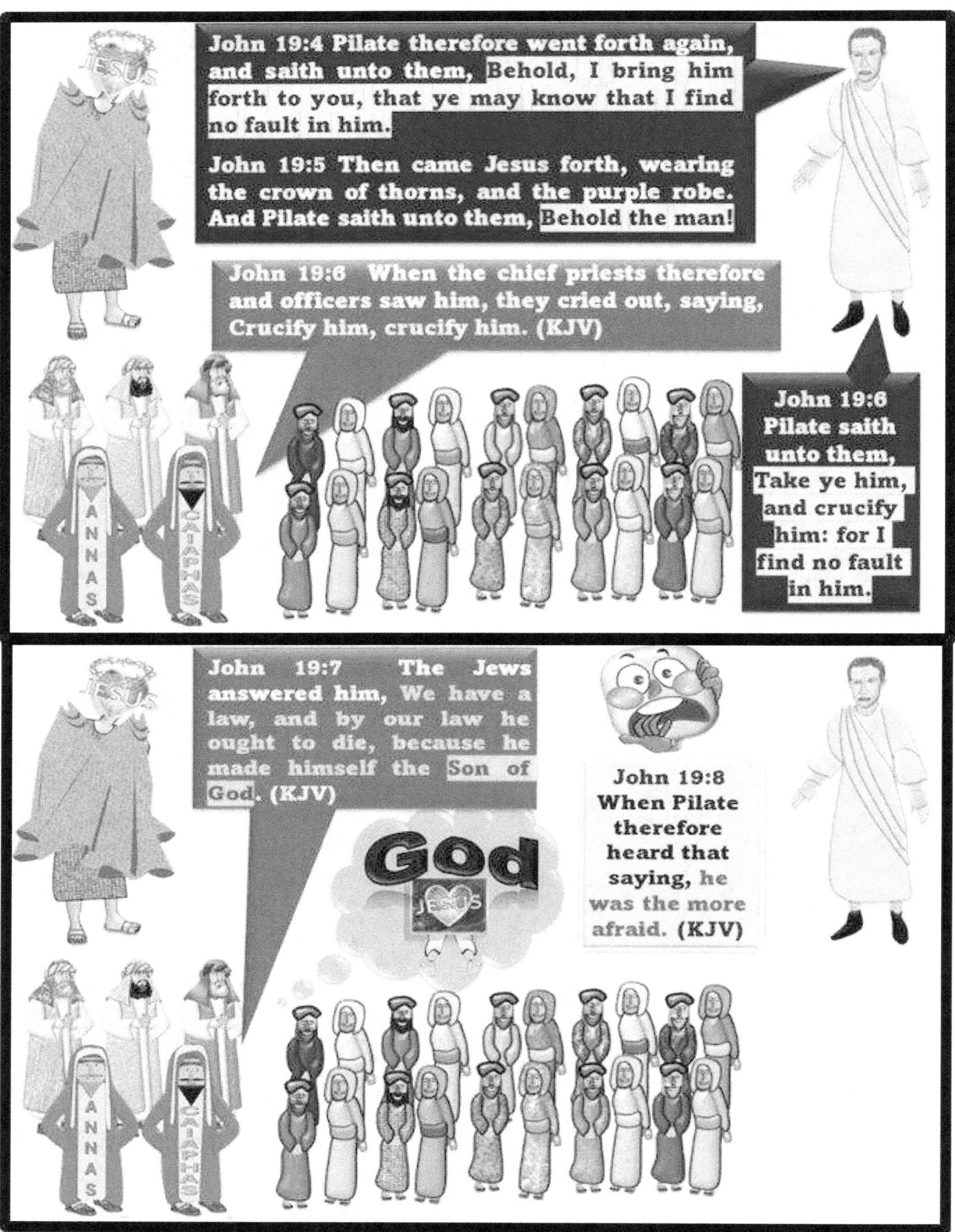

John 19:4 Pilate therefore went forth again, and saith unto them, Behold, I bring him forth to you, that ye may know that I find no fault in him.

John 19:5 Then came Jesus forth, wearing the crown of thorns, and the purple robe. And Pilate saith unto them, Behold the man!

John 19:6 When the chief priests therefore and officers saw him, they cried out, saying, Crucify him, crucify him. (KJV)

John 19:6 Pilate saith unto them, Take ye him, and crucify him: for I find no fault in him.

John 19:7 The Jews answered him, We have a law, and by our law he ought to die, because he made himself the Son of God. (KJV)

God
JESUS

John 19:8 When Pilate therefore heard that saying, he was the more afraid. (KJV)

Here are the Bible verses that describe the incident where the Roman soldiers shoved a Crown of Thorns upon the head of Our Lord, a robe on His back, and pretended to worship Jesus. With His hands tied, Jesus had no way to wipe away the blood that would be trickling down His face.

6th Trial for Jesus – 2nd time with Pilate

Matthew 27:29-31	Mark 15:17-20	Luke	John 19:2-3
29 When they had twisted a crown of thorns, they put it on His head, and a reed in His right hand. And they bowed the knee before Him and mocked Him, saying, "Hail, King of the Jews!" 30 Then they spat on Him, and took the reed and struck Him on the head. 31 And when they had mocked Him, they took the robe off Him, put His own clothes on Him, and led Him away to be crucified.	17 They put a purple robe on him, then twisted together a crown of thorns and set it on him. 18 And they began to call out to him, "Hail, king of the Jews!" 19 Again and again they struck him on the head with a staff and spit on him. Falling on their knees, they paid homage to him. 20 And when they had mocked him, they took off the purple robe and put his own clothes on him. Then they led him out to crucify him.	No Reference to this Topic 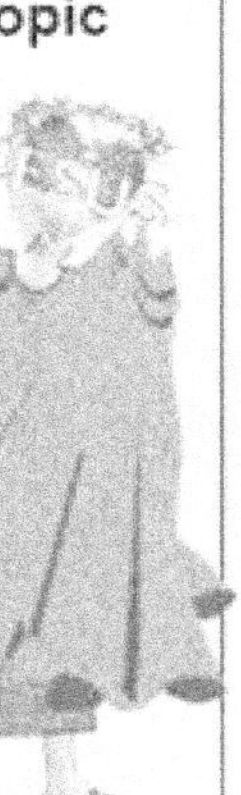	2 And the soldiers platted a crown of thorns, and put it on his head, and they put on him a purple robe, 3 And said, Hail, King of the Jews! and they smote him with their hands.

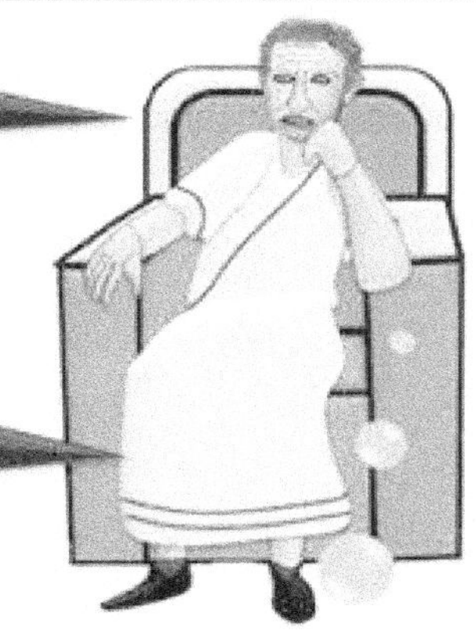

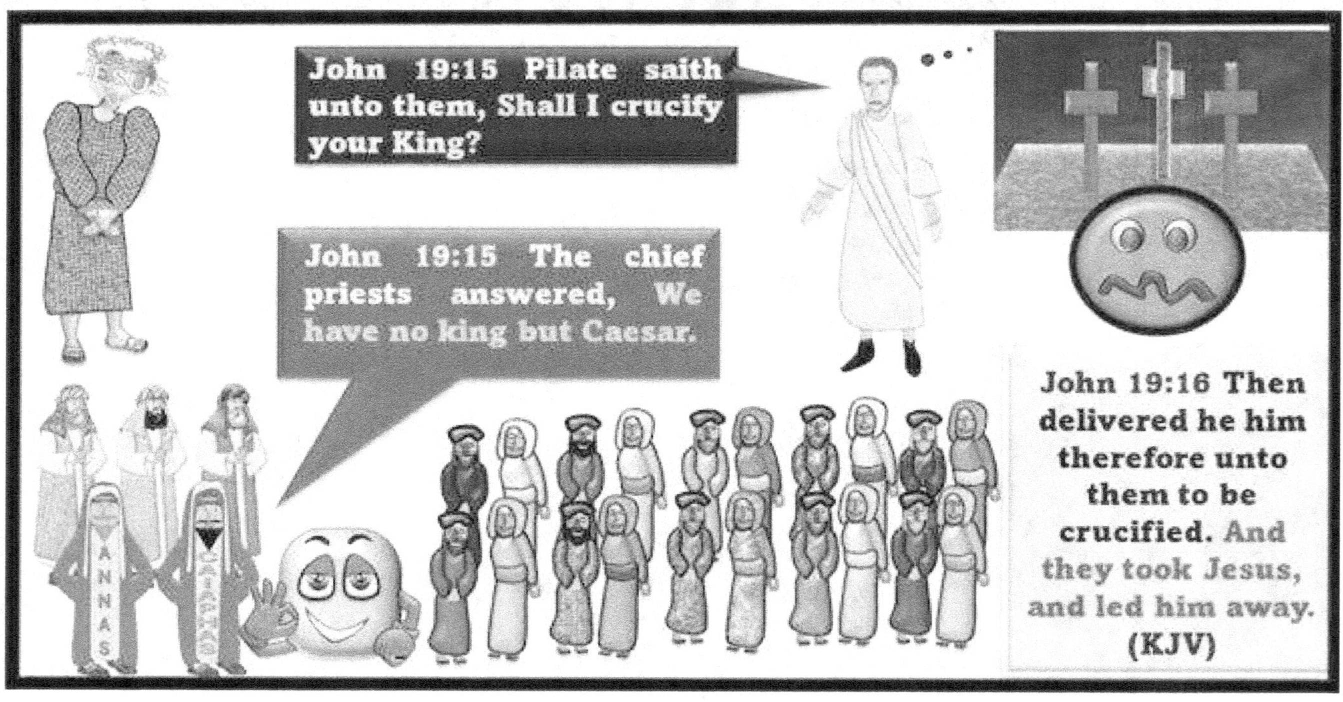

John 19:12 And from thenceforth Pilate sought to release him: but the Jews cried out, saying, If thou let this man go, thou art not Caesar's friend: whosoever maketh himself a king speaketh against Caesar.

John 19:13 When Pilate therefore heard that saying, he brought Jesus forth, and sat down in the judgment seat in a place that is called the Pavement, but in the Hebrew, Gabbatha. (KJV)

John 19:14 And it was the preparation of the passover, and about the sixth hour: and he saith unto the Jews, Behold your King!

John 19:15 But they cried out, Away with him, away with him, crucify him.

ANNAS
CAIAPHAS

John 19:15 Pilate saith unto them, Shall I crucify your King?

John 19:15 The chief priests answered, We have no king but Caesar.

John 19:16 Then delivered he him therefore unto them to be crucified. And they took Jesus, and led him away. (KJV)

ANNAS
CAIAPHAS

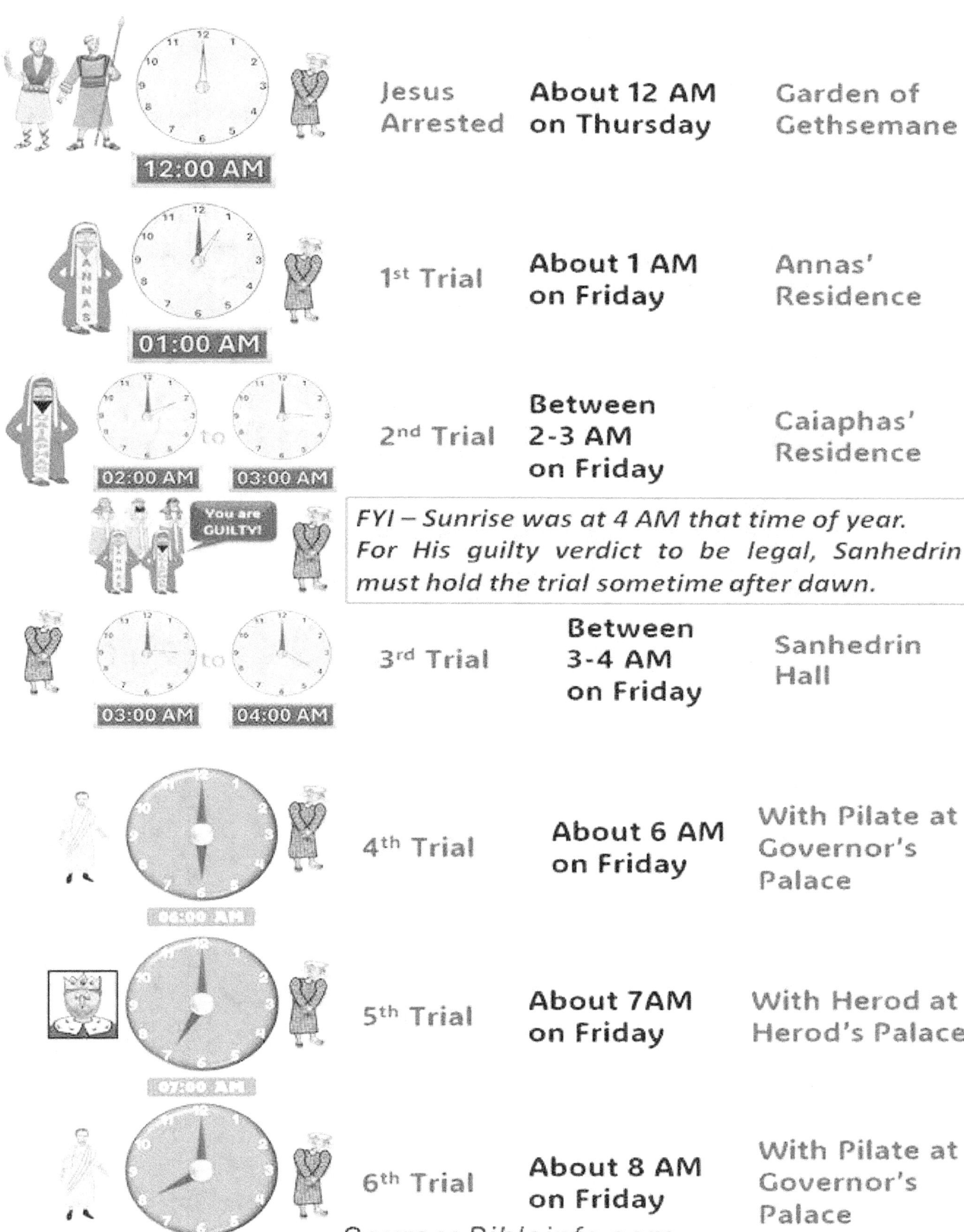

Jesus Arrested	**About 12 AM on Thursday**	Garden of Gethsemane
1st Trial	**About 1 AM on Friday**	Annas' Residence
2nd Trial	**Between 2-3 AM on Friday**	Caiaphas' Residence
3rd Trial	**Between 3-4 AM on Friday**	Sanhedrin Hall
4th Trial	**About 6 AM on Friday**	With Pilate at Governor's Palace
5th Trial	**About 7AM on Friday**	With Herod at Herod's Palace
6th Trial	**About 8 AM on Friday**	With Pilate at Governor's Palace

> *FYI – Sunrise was at 4 AM that time of year. For His guilty verdict to be legal, Sanhedrin must hold the trial sometime after dawn.*

Source: Bibleinfo.com

What was the punishment of scourging?
What were the effects of Roman scourging?

"For scourging, the man was stripped of his clothing, and his hands were tied to an upright post. The back, buttocks, and legs were flogged either by two soldiers (lictors [i.e., officers]) or by one who alternated positions." … "A Roman soldier would strike the victim 39 times with a whip whose leather straps were laced with slivers of sharp bones and small metal balls that severely cut into the body, exposing bones and internal organs. Many victims, severely injured and bleeding, would die during the scourging."

Jesus was stripped naked, arms raised above His head, tied to a rough, wooden post, and whipped 39 to 40 times with a Flagellum, also known as a Cat o' nine tails. Two Roman soldiers alternated whipping Him so hard that the skin of His back and lower backside would have been left in shreds, and parts of His bones and internal organs would have been visible for all eyes to see. This scourging was part of the punishment Jesus lovingly and graciously took in our place to save us from suffering in hell for our many sins, large and small.

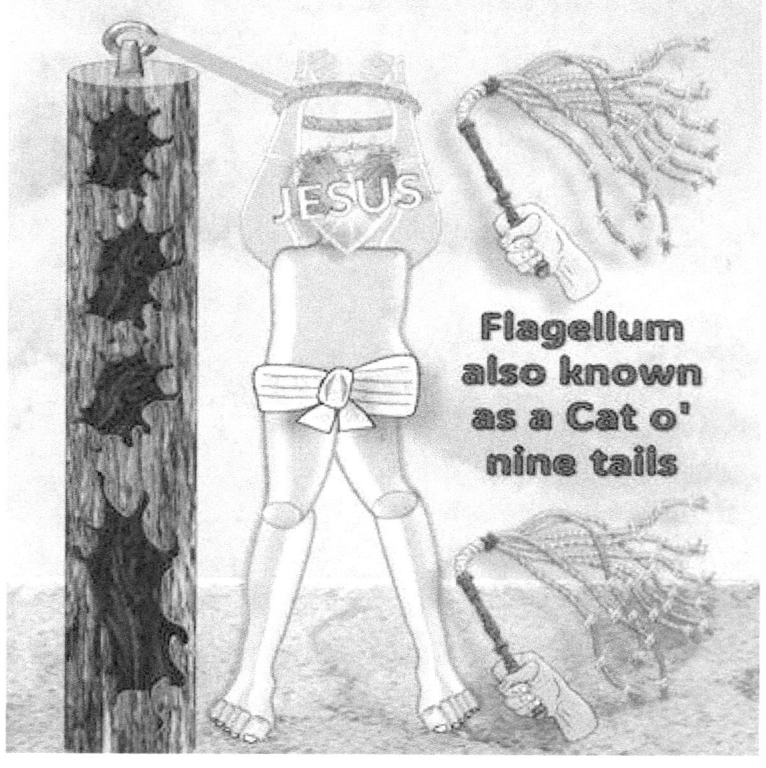

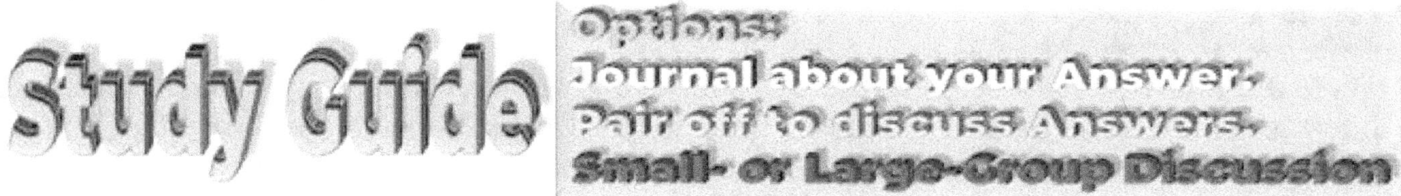

1. When describing Jesus, what did the Pharisees say to Pilate?

2. What did Pilate learn from Jesus during this meeting?

3. What was the dream that Pilate's wife have? What did she try to convince her husband to do as a result of this dream?

4. What prevented Pilate from doing what his wife requested?

5. What were two reasons Pilate sent Jesus to Herod?

6. What happened when Jesus met with Herod?

7. In Pilate's second meeting with Jesus, what do you think he was convinced or convicted about?

8. The Bible verses of Matthew 27:18 and Mark 15:10 state that Pilate realized it was **ENVY** that most motivated the Pharisees to want to see Jesus dead. What do you think the Pharisees were envious about?

9. Why do you think Pilate agreed to do what the Pharisees requested?

10. Do you think washing his hands really cleansed Pilate of the sin of agreeing to put Jesus to death?

11. What tortures did the Roman soldiers administer to Jesus?

12. Why do you think the people preferred to have Barabbas set free rather than Jesus?

13. What was the end result of all six trials?

14. Describe the timeline of when each event happened: Last Supper, Jesus' prayers in garden, Judas' kiss, arrest, first trial with Annas, second trail with Caiaphas, third trial with Sanhedrin, fourth trial with Pilate, fifth trial with Herod, the scourging and other tortures , and the sixth trial with Pilate.

Author's Dedication

There are many ways to demonstrate our love for and worship of our Lord Jesus Christ. This book is a rendering of data points for you to prayerfully consider that might give your worship of Him a deeper dimension. I dedicate this book to all honest seekers of truth. May it provide another viewing point of the **WORD** in the Holy Bible.

Author's Acknowledgements

There was a deeper purpose for authoring this book. I wrote this book not for my glory but for the glory of our Heavenly God the Father, God the Son, and God the Holy Spirit. I am so grateful for all the manifold ways God, the **Trinity of three Persons**, continually blesses my life. May this book bless your life, as well.

I acknowledge and am so grateful for all the people who created the Bible APPS, Google, Microsoft PowerPoint, Microsoft Word, the Paint APP, books, videos, movies, talks, and sermons that fed my imagination and blessed my life. I also acknowledge the countless moments of comfort and blessings I receive from my dear and treasured family and friends (both living and deceased), of which I count you, my readers, among them. I am eternally grateful! God bless you all! May you have a blessed and touched-by-God life!

Final Blessings

I find myself speculating if God planted me exactly where He did and gave me all the experiences that He gave me just so I could write this book.

And then I feel the **Holy Spirit** nudging me, reminding me of this Bible verse:

Romans 8:28 And we know that all things work together for good to them that love God, to them who are called according to his purpose. (KJV)

May the **Holy Spirit** touch and bless you, as well, and help you to fulfill the mission that God has prescribed just for you.

I end this book with two final blessings, one by King David, the other by Moses.

Psalm 121:8 The Lord keeps watch over you as you come and go, both now and forever. (NLT)

Numbers 6:24 The LORD bless you and keep you. 25 The LORD make his face shine upon you and be gracious to you. 26 The LORD turn his face toward you and give you peace. (NIV)

AMEN. Thank you for making the time to read a part or all of this book. Kindly consider leaving a review, even if it is only a sentence or two.

Also, if you found it pleasing, please share this book with the people you love.

BIBLIOGRAPHY

Bibliography: Used for entire book

Bible Gateway.com. (October 2023 to May 2024). Read the Bible. Website; https://www.biblegateway.com/

Developer Unknown. (October 2023 to May 2024). Bible – Daily Bible Verse KJV. From a free cell phone APP.

Google.com Search Engine. (October 2023 to May 2024).

Grammarly.com for editing (October 2023 to May 2024).

Kairos Software LLC. Developer. (October 2023 to May 2024). Bible KJV Strong's Concordance. From a free cell phone APP. (October – November 2023)

On-line dictionary via Google Search Engine. (October 2023 to May 2024).

Bibliography: Resources to increase my understanding

Abbott, Shari for Reasons for Hope * Jesus. (January 2024). Did Pilate Proclaim Jesus to be God? A Remez on the Cross. Website: https://reasonsforhopejesus.com/pilate-proclaimed-jesus-god/

Adams, Heather for Bible Study Tools.com. (November 2023). What Is Hyssop and Why Is It so Significant in the Bible? Website: https://www.biblestudytools.com/bible-study/topical-studies/what-is-hyssop-and-why-is-it-so-significant-in-the-bible.html

Colón, Peter for Israel My Glory.org. (February 2024). The Feast of Tabernacles in the Days of Jesus. Website: https://israelmyglory.org/article/the-feast-of-tabernacles-in-the-days-of-jesus/

Colton, John for Frog.org. (January 2024). Did Pilate Proclaim Jesus to be God as Well as King of the Jews? Website: https://www.frog.org.nz/johns-blog/179

Cooke, Tony. (November 2023). Medical Description of the Flogging and Crucifixion of Jesus. Website: https://tonycooke.org/articles-by-tony-cooke/medical-description-jesus/

Doron, Reuven for Sarel Tours.com. (November 2023). The Complete Guide to The Garden of Gethsemane. Website: https://sareltours.com/article/the-garden-of-gethsemane

Gardner, Ryan S. (February 2024). Jesus Christ and the Feast of Tabernacles. Website: https://rsc.byu.edu/vol-13-no-3-2012/jesus-christ-feast-tabernacles

Got Questions.org. (February 2024). What did Jesus mean when He said "I AM"? Website: https://www.gotquestions.org/I-AM.html

Got Questions.org. (November 2023). What is the significance of thirty pieces of silver? Website: https://www.gotquestions.org/thirty-pieces-of-silver.html

Got Questions.org. (January 2024). What time was Jesus crucified? Website: https://www.gotquestions.org/what-time-was-Jesus-crucified.html

Grace Transcending the Torah.com. (April 2024). Feasts of the Lord. Website: https://www.gracetranscendingthetorah.com/feasts/

Hunt, Michal for Agape Bible Study.com. (March 2024). PLAN OF THE TABERNACLE. Website: https://www.agapebiblestudy.com/charts/Plan%20of%20the%20Tabernacle.htm

Hunt, Michael for Agape Bible Study. (January 2024). Twelve-Hour Daylight Division: The Hours of Prayer for the Old Covenant Church. Website: https://www.agapebiblestudy.com/charts/jewishtimedivision.htm

Kantor, Mattis for Chabad.org. (November 2023). Timeline of Jewish History. Website: https://www.chabad.org/library/article_cdo/aid/3915966/jewish/Timeline-of-Jewish-History.htm

King James Bible Online.org. (January 2024). 2 Esdras 2:26. Website: https://www.kingjamesbibleonline.org/2-Esdras-2-26/

Lizorkin-Eyzenberg, Dr. Eliyahu. (January 2024). The Hidden Hebrew Message on the Pilate's Cross. Website: https://weekly.israelbiblecenter.com/hidden-hebrew-message-pilates-cross

Messages of Christ on YouTube. (February 2024). Understanding Feast of Tabernacles or Sukkot. Video length: 9:23 minutes. Website: https://www.youtube.com/watch?v=u6PmxypqZ9I

One for Israel.org. (November 2023). The Untold Reason why Jewish People do not believe Jesus is the Messiah! Website: https://www.oneforisrael.org/bible-based-teaching-from-israel/the-untold-reason-why-jewish-people-do-not-believe-jesus-is-the-messiah/

Ramgopal and Arte for Presentation Process. (November 2023). How To Create Beautiful Chain Graphic in PowerPoint. Website: https://www.youtube.com/watch?v=jjioPJ-_gIk

Ramgopal and Arte for Presentation Process. (October 2023). How to Create Clock Needle Animation Effect in PowerPoint. Produced by Presentation Process. Website: https://www.youtube.com/watch?v=3XVrJnFok88&t=267s

Scripture Central on YouTube. (February 2024). The Feast of Tabernacles (Come, Follow Me: John 7). Video length: 3:48 minutes. Website: https://www.youtube.com/watch?v=dOL4rps-s5E

St. Mary Mystical Rose Catholic Community.org. February 2024). The Six Trials of Jesus Christ. Website: https://stmarymysticalrose.org/six-trials-of-jesus-christ

The Bible Nerds. (December 2023). Remez: A Hint For Better Bible Study. Website: https://thebiblenerds.com/remez-a-hint-for-better-bible-study/

Understand Christianity.com. (February 2024). Chronology of Jesus' Life and Ministry. Website: https://www.understandchristianity.com/timelines/chronology-jesus-life-ministry/

Westover, Jeff for My Merry Christmas.com. (January 2024). The History of Santa Claus is Coming to Town. Website: https://mymerrychristmas.com/the-history-of-santa-claus-is-coming-to-town/

Wikipedia.org. (January 2024). 2 Esdras. Website: https://en.wikipedia.org/wiki/2_Esdras

Wikipedia.org. (January 2024). Gethsemane. Website: https://en.wikipedia.org/wiki/Gethsemane

Wikipedia.org. (March 2024). Judas Iscariot. Website: https://en.wikipedia.org/wiki/Judas_Iscariot

Wikipedia.org. (January 2024). Recording angel. Website: https://en.wikipedia.org/wiki/Recording_angel

Winger, Mike on YouTube. (April 2024). The Spring Feasts of Israel: How to Find Jesus in the OT pt 21. Website: https://youtu.be/A-_6rpQ4zLg?si=ifsM5bWnjma82pH0

Zavada, Jack (Christianity expert). (March 2024). Meet Caiaphas: High Priest of the Jerusalem Temple. Website: https://www.learnreligions.com/caiaphas-high-priest-of-the-jerusalem-temple-701058